The Judgment of Paris

Books of related interest

Contemporary Cultural Theory
Andrew Miller

Heterology and the Post Modern
Bataille, Baudrillard and Lyotard
Julian Pefanis

Jacques Lacan
A feminist introduction
Elizabeth Grosz

Sexual Subversions
Three French feminists
Elizabeth Grosz

THE JUDGMENT OF PARIS

Recent French theory in a local context

Edited by
Kevin D. S. Murray

ALLEN & UNWIN

First published in 1992
Allen & Unwin Pty Ltd
8 Napier Street, North Sydney, NSW 2059, Australia

National Library of Australia
Cataloguing-in-Publication entry:

The judgment of Paris: recent French theory in a local context.

Includes index.
ISBN 1 86373 055 9.

1. Philosophy, French—20th century. 2. France—Intellectual life— 20th
century. I. Murray, Kevin D.

194

Set in 10.5/11.5 Sabon by Adtype Graphics Pty Ltd, North Sydney
Printed by Chong Moh Offset Printing Private Limited, Singapore

Contents

Contributors

PETER COTTON is in the Deptartment of History and Philsophy of Science at the University of Melbourne. He is also a clinical psychologist and maintains a private practice in psychotherapy.

KEVIN HART is Associate Professor of Critical Theory at Monash University. He teaches in the Department of English and the Centre for General and Comparative Literature. His most recent theoretical publication is *The Trespass of the Sign: Deconstruction, Theology and Philosophy* (Cambridge University Press, 1989). His latest collection of poetry is *Peniel* (Golvan Arts Press, 1991).

HENRY KRIPS occupies the Chair in the Department of Communication, University of Pittsburg. When writing for this volume, he was Reader in the History and Philosophy of Science Department, University of Melbourne. He has recently published *The Metaphysics of Quantum Theory* (Clarendon Press, 1990), and he is currently working on a book about rhetoric in science.

BRENDA LUDEMAN is a writer of fiction and art criticism; her work has been well published in local art magazines and she is pursuing a project about presenting text in the public space.

CHRIS McAULIFFE is a doctoral candidate at Harvard University where he is researching the place of French theory in the development of American postmodernism. He teaches art history at the University of Melbourne and is co-publisher of *Rebus*, a magazine of artists' pages.

KEVIN MURRAY is a freelance writer and curator. He has completed a PhD on the subject of life construction and overseas travel. Murray has co-ordinated four series of talks about contemporary culture (papers from *Foreign Knowledge* published in *Tension* 21, 1990).

DAVID ODELL has a PhD in Mathematics from Cornell. He has a long-standing interest in literary theory and is translating for publication certain works of Blanchot. One of his main interests is the process of reflection involved in the act of writing. He looks at Blanchot's position in both Hegelian philosophy and modernist fiction.

JULIAN PEFANIS is a lecturer in Visual Culture of the Twentieth Century at the Power Institute, University of Sydney. He is author of *Heterology and the Postmodern* and has translated several works by French authors, including Jean Baudrillard (*Revenge of the Crystal*), Pierre Clastres ('On Ethnocide') and J. F. Lyotard (*The Thought Police*). He is currently editing a collection of essays by J. F. Lyotard (*The Postmodern Explained for Children*).

CLARE O'FARRELL teaches Sociology at Brisbane CAE; she is the author of a book on Foucault (Macmillan, 1990). In 1988 she was visiting scholar working with Bourdieu at *Science de la Muse de l'Homme*.

VIRGINIA TRIOLI is a writer and works as a journalist for the Melbourne *Age*.

Preface

The contributions in this volume have been collected with three kinds of readers in mind. Those who are uninitiated in particular French authors may find these essays a useful introduction to their works, particularly as they are apprehended in the contemporary scene. Readers who consider themselves read in those authors might approach the essays as original contributions to the nature of French thought: the essays are not intended simply as digestible substitutes for the original writers, but as unique demonstrations of the degree to which their works can be put into practice. And finally, those who wish to reflect on the significance of Parisian ideas in an English-speaking culture will find essays which both bring the issue of context into focus and make personal claims for its relevance.

This publication is based on a series of talks held on Saturday evenings in August–November 1988, at a public gallery in Melbourne, 200 Gertrude Street Artists Space and Gallery. For many this was a critical period in formulating a defence of intellectual practice. It was around this time that 'public accountability' became more than a rhetorical cry around the universities. It was an environment which called for demonstrations of relevance that were different from the simplistic economic indices then governing most debates about the rationalisation of the universities. Fortunately, there existed a number of local individuals who had dedicated a great deal to understanding particular recent French writers and were willing to stand before a non-academic audience in order to test their relevance outside the university.

The emergence of this volume has relied on a number of people who are confident in the possibility of local thought. Louise Neri began by opening up 200 Gertrude Street to unfashionably dressed academics and bringing the seminar into the art gallery. After the success of the 'Judgment of Paris' series, Chris Wallace-Crabbe, Paul Carter and Rose Lang pushed along the idea of publication. At this time, the actions and talk of Virginia Trioli and Philippa Hawker were critical in maintaining its impetus. Conversations with Geoff Lowe and David Odell provided valuable feedback for the ideas that introduce the volume. As it began to come to light, Deborah Edwards, Bruce James and Naomi Cass were very generous with their services in tracking down an Australian image of 'Judgment of Paris'. And at the critical moments, John Iremonger, and Rhonda Black and Bernadette Foley at Allen & Unwin have helped steady the course towards a future readership.

KEVIN MURRAY

Introduction

> It is the spirit of social life which develops a thinking mind, and
> carries the eye as far as it can reach. If you have a spark of genius,
> go and spend a year in Paris; you will soon be all that you are
> capable of becoming, or you will never be good for anything at all.
>
> Jean-Jacques Rousseau[1]

Recent thought from Paris has experienced surprising popularity in
the English-speaking world. Highbrow bookshops and university
reading lists are filled with titles by Derrida, Kristeva, Foucault and
their ilk. Now that these names have established themselves, it is
appropriate to reflect on what kind of impression has been made by
recent French theory, and whether it has been a good thing.

Clearly, there are some who will doubt its worth. A certain kind of
reader approaches a book on recent French theory with great scepticism. The thoughts are: 'It's all dressed up to sound intelligent, but
does it really have anything to say?'; 'All this Parisian theory is just a
passing fashion—let's get back to plain, unadorned common sense'.
This kind of reader is suspicious of appearances: you can't judge a
book by its cover. While the present volume welcomes a reader such
as this—happy to have its arguments tested out against a 'real world'
of facts and reason—it is hoped that this reader will remain aware of
the specific nature of the kind of reading being used. Simulation/
reality, fashion/history, theories/facts—it is exactly these kinds of
difference which are the subject of critical attention in much recent
French theory. These kinds of difference concern the distinction
between appearance and essence: the dustjacket and the contents of
the book. There is much of modern life which still rests on this
difference: for example, the position of psychotherapist often

depends upon the notion of a hidden self that lies obscured by surface personality. This 'getting to know the *real* person' is one of the many places where the difference attended to by the French between simulation and authenticity has relevance to everyday life—academic debate need not be its sole domain of application.

The purpose of this volume is to examine the products of this attention in English- and French-speaking settings. It makes a link between the ideas and their contexts in French and Anglo cultures. The difference between these two cultures has often been stereotyped: while the English are traditionally known as favouring practical forms of life, the French are seen to license ostentation. Ralph Waldo Emerson compared English and French couture along similar lines: while the French invented the ruffle, the English added the shirt.[2] One strives to appear different and the other just gets on with the job.

In this introduction I'd like to adopt the stereotyped shirt-making Anglo as a background to understanding how recent French thought might be evaluated. This evaluation is not based on the formal truth-values attached to ideas from Paris, but on the cultural space they have established for themselves in English-speaking countries—not whether recent French theory offers a replacement for the Anglo picture of things, but how it is incorporated into this picture. Derrida's concept of *différance* and Kristeva's attention to the *semiotic* are both examples of moments in French theory which attend to the packaging of meaning—moments that might be simplified in the axiom: though you can't judge a book by its cover, you need the cover as a means of containing the essence of the book. In Paris, normal relations of meaning are overturned: repetition comes first, we are spoken by language, and logic is just an accident.

This French thought is alien to our common sense. How does an Anglo reader deal with it? Should it be dismissed as fancy intellectual footwork or be taken as a serious challenge to deeply held values? How a reader deals with this question will depend partly on how they regard things French. The purpose of this introduction is to construct pictures of French culture which present alternative forms of negotiation: opening up to it as a language for revealing the invisible ground on which common sense operates, or closing the door on it as a foreign currency in which only the elite can speculate. This is a Paris pictured alternatively as a *lamp* which reveals the world outside it, or a *bonfire* that makes a spectacle of itself.

THE LAMP OF TRUTH

The status of Paris as intellectual centre is by no means unique to the modern world. The life of the thirteenth-century Catalan theologian Ramon Llull provides a sense of the power of Paris when very different ideas held sway. Ramon Llull is a precursor of Leibniz: it was Llull who first conceived the possibility of a philosophical machine that could account for the nature of the world in terms of a limited number of logical operations. While Leibniz designed his *Ars Combinatoria* for use within an academic context, Llull's theological diagrams were reproduced as illuminated manuscripts, intended by their colour and simplicity to convert Saracens to the Catholic faith. After spending many years perfecting his theoretical system, Llull travelled unassisted to Moslem countries and presented his arguments in their marketplaces. At 75 years of age, he enraged the Moslems of the North African city of Bougie by contesting their beliefs in a public square. When summoned before the Mohammedan bishop for what seemed certain execution, he continued his case for the existence of the Holy Trinity, confident that the bishop's erroneous belief would crumble when confronted with reason. Llull was very lucky to escape with only prison and torture; no one, in the end, listened.

Where did Llull gain this confidence in the strengths of philosophical argument? While other Christian warriors were mustering their forces in England and Rome, Llull chose to take his authority from the city considered to be the centre of reason: Paris. Llull described Paris in a letter to Philippe Le Bel in 1287:

> O fountain of supernatural wisdom, which has made drunk with marvellous doctrine so many teachers of Paris, [who are endowed] with such authority! ... Happy is that University which has brought forth so many defenders of the Faith and happy that city whose soldiers armed with the wisdom and devotion of Christ, are able to subdue barbarous nations to the Supreme King. [It is in Paris] where the source of divine learning springs up, whence the *lamp of truth* shines forth. From thee light goes forth to all peoples; thou shalt sound out the witness to truth, and to thee shall come masters and disciples from all and all shall drink from thee the knowledge of every science.[3]

In Ramon Llull's world, Paris acted as a fulcrum for the power of divine disputation: it was the ground of truth on which he could lever his arguments. As a theological centre, the force of Paris was seen to radiate outwards, giving strength of argument to those who quested to extend the Christian empire.

In today's world, Lull's picture of Paris as a 'lamp of truth' seems based on both an idealisation of the city and an imperialist understanding of knowledge. The alternative to 'lamp of truth' looks in the opposite direction. Paris here is a self-absorbed city turned towards its own spectacle, indifferent to the world around it. Earlier this century, Paul Valéry's account of the 'delirious professions' that are conducted in Paris shows a city which is carried away with itself:

> There is no place on earth, I thought, where language has greater frequency, more resonance, less reserve than in this very Paris where the literature, the sciences, the arts and politics of a great country are jealously concentrated. The French have stored all their ideas in one enclosure. Here we live in our own fire ... Just think of the temperature that may be reached in a place where so great a number of *prides* are comparing themselves to one another. Paris contains and combines, and consummates or consumes, most of the brilliant failures summoned by their destinies to the *delirious professions* ... This tribe of *uniques* is ruled by the law of doing what no one has ever done and no one will ever do. This at least is the law of the *best*—that is, of those who have the pluck to will something obviously absurd.[4]

Valéry's description makes intellectual life in Paris seem like some wild fashion parade—it is a fire in which the brightest survives briefly while the rest of the world looks on. The 'lamp of truth' which Llull used to guide his mission has here turned into an intellectual *bonfire*. The fire operates as an amusement that defies order, not as a guide for others. In Valéry's picture, intellectual difference is promoted for its own sake rather than for the sake of reason. The consequence of this picture is that such ideas are not to be taken seriously. This opinion is cast in a more recent context by Emmanuel Lévinas, a foreign-born philosopher living in Paris, who wrote in 1950:

> The end of humanism, of metaphysics, the death of man, the death of God (or death to God!)—these are apocalyptic ideas or slogans of intellectual high society. Like all the manifestations of Parisian taste (or Parisian disgusts), these topics impose themselves with the tyranny of the last word, but become available to anyone and cheapened.[5]

In this picture, though Paris might seem to deliver ideas of astounding historical depth, they turn out to be simply forms of intellectual scandal designed to titillate the crowds.

So these are two kinds of pictures for treating ideas from Paris: as a lamp that illuminates the rest of the world, or as a bonfire that draws the world's attention to itself. One treats Paris seriously, the other not. Despite this difference, both pictures place that city at a distance from the rest of the world. Paris is where knowledge glows brightest—it just depends whether you are looking towards it or away from it.

At this point, our stereotyped Anglo reader is likely to cry foul: surely you cannot confuse the ideas that emanate from Paris with the uses that are made of them. Ideas should be judged independently of their cultural ownership—that a machine is made by a foreign power has nothing to do with its standards of performance. This protest, however, defers to an abstract notion of ideas which does not allow for their interaction with local conditions of thought. Clearly, that certain ideas have certain uses in Paris does not limit their application elsewhere. However, for an idea to work it must find some purpose with which to engage.

THE LIFE OF AN IDEA

The reception of schools of thought by cultures foreign to their originating context need not be seen as simply an attempt to import a system of knowledge intact: ideas are not necessarily free agents able to look after themselves. The 'adequation' theory of ideas claims that objects of thought are prior to the ideas we have of them: thought has no life itself, it simply mimics what already exists. But this does not account for the possibility that ideas might have a life of their own, particularly as they are used to construct different versions of a world. An alternative way of looking at the 'idea' is given by the Russian theorist Mikhail Bakhtin, who provides the maxim: 'The idea is a live event'.[6] Bakhtin proposed that the idea is an utterance to be understood within a dialogical context. He demonstrated this in the novels of Dostoevsky, where characters are presented as beings who attempt to 'get a thought straight'. The idea becomes embodied in consciousness:

> As it loses its monologic, abstractly theoretical finalised quality, a quality sufficient to a *single* consciousness, it acquires the contradictory complexity and living multi-facedness of an idea-force, being born, living and acting in the great dialogue of the epoch and calling back and forth to kindred ideas of other epochs. Before us rises up an *image of the idea*.[7]

For us, Dostoevsky's novels demonstrate how European philosophy became personified in the life of the 1860s declassé Russian intellectual: they show how an idea such as 'everything is permissible', born of a French-speaking local aristocracy, fell into argument with

Russian Orthodoxy and radical popularism. But where is a Dostoevsky *now* to write of the destiny of contemporary French thought in the lives of English-speaking intellectuals?

What is available mostly takes the form of satire, such as the comic novels by English academics David Lodge and Malcolm Bradbury. Such satire sees the recent manifestation of French theory as not worth taking seriously, and as such may seem not worth taking seriously itself in this discussion. However, the kind of comic space which it makes available for French theory represents one kind of opening for alternative thought in the English-speaking academies. For this reason, their comedy is worth taking seriously.

Malcolm Bradbury's novel *Mensonge* is one such satire on recent French thought. Bradbury presents a fictionalised case of the greatest French deconstructor, who, true to his theory of authorship, has destroyed all traces of his ideas. While the plot cleverly points to some of the paradoxes of a deconstructive practice, it is the tone of the writing which has most to say about the treatment of French theory. *Mensonge* associates recent French theory with a chic world:

> Today it would be foolish, or decidedly unsmart, to attend any congress or cocktail party in the great cities of the world, and not be able to parry a Lacan with a Derrida, lead with Foucault and follow up with a Kristeva.[8]

Bradbury's satiric portrait reflects an Anglo reader looking sceptically on the high fashion of French theory. There is a difference between the English satire and the scepticism acknowledged by the Parisians themselves: while ideas in Paris are prized for their rarity, the same ideas in England are used as signs of social inclusion. While in Paris it is the desire to be different which holds sway (Valéry's 'tribe of *uniques*'), in Bradbury's version of the English-speaking academic world, the governing motive is to be a member of the same knowing group. The butt of Bradbury's satire is the socialite who acquires a new French idea simply because it supports their claim to belong to the clique.

How seriously should one take this satire? What if it were true that French theory was taken up in the English-speaking world as a phenomenon of intellectual fashion? Is it fair to judge French theory simply according to the uses that are made of it? This is certainly not a rare process: one is more likely now to evaluate nationalism by its uses in the twentieth century (for example, Nazism) than by its logical coherence. However, there is the sense that a serious examination of French thought should take place on a formal level—not at the cocktail party but in the seminar room. Without denying the importance of an institution that is removed from the 'real world', I want to claim that the academic world is inappropriate for the evaluation of French theory presented in this volume.

IDEAS IN AN ACADEMIC WORLD

It is a paradox of the academic world that it denies its worldliness. The official picture of ideas occludes their sensitivity to context: they are seen ideally as 'immutable mobiles'[9] that freely circulate around the globe expanding the base of universal knowledge. How are ideas freed from their ecological niches? In *Institution and Interpretation*, Samuel Weber presents a description which is of some use to us here. Weber claims that the university provides the mediation which turns local knowledge into professionalised knowledge. He describes the university:

> It was and remains the gateway to the professions, marking the transition from the local, geographically determined community of youth, centred around the family, to that 'translocal' academic community, structured in terms of the professional disciplines themselves.[10]

Within the English-speaking liberal academic tradition, ideas are not generally associated with specific rhetorical conditions: they are judged in the light of individual reason. Because of this, the recent success within these universities of a set of ideas antagonistic to the ground of individual subjectivity has a certain irony. Weber describes the 'price' paid by these ideas in the English-speaking context:

> If authors such as Derrida, Foucault, and, to a lesser extent, Lacan, have been granted admission into the American Academy, the price they have had to pay has generally entailed the universalisation and individualisation of their work, which has thereby been purged of its conflictual and strategic elements and presented instead as a self-standing methodology.[11]

This is the central irony of the dissemination of recent French thought into an English-speaking academic world: *that an intellectual movement which stresses the dependence of meaning on context should be adopted so successfully without consideration of its own context.*

There are already signs of impatience with French post-structuralism. This comes not from a lack of faith in the ideas of the movement, but rather as a response to its disconcerting success. How does an apparently *subversive* theory account for its acceptance as *orthodoxy* within the academic community? This problem has not escaped the notice of American deconstructors, such as Barbara Johnson.[12] Johnson advises against feeling 'comfortable in the abyss'; she claims this complacency counters the 'surprise of otherness' which is the most tangible expression of an imperative in deconstructive reading practices. To counter this she promotes a form of intellectual ignorance: forget the edifice of learning accumulated in the name of deconstruction and think again! While this strategy might be useful in maintaining the vivacity of deconstruction within academic life, this form of forgetting is much less forced when one confronts the problem of its assimilation in a local context.[13]

THE MOVEABLE FEAST

A successful academic practice is established through the annual round of overseas conferences and regular contact with international journals. The university lifestyle requires the routine maintenance of global links that can connect a lecturer in Sociology at Sydney University with what they are saying about deconstruction at Yale University. In this picture, 'Paris' may simply be seen as one of the world's leading laboratories, producing the latest innovations in argumentative technique. This 'Paris' need not be in France; it could be *anywhere*.

This picture is a plainly inadequate representation of what Paris signifies in English-speaking cultures. Indeed, it is an attempt to obscure the unique voice established for Paris through centuries of travel and cultural exchange.[14] Emerson wrote of France that it served as 'a kind of blackboard on which English character draws its own traits in chalk'.[15] What does this blackboard say to us now?

An alternative picture of knowledge opposes the abstract community of academics to more locally constituted cultural groups. But this is uncharted water, and we are unsure of its depths. A sign of this uncertainty would be to claim that the 'international market' of ideas has removed the possibility of regional schools of thought—has not communication technology more truly brought home the adage that Paris is a 'moveable feast'? However, to raise this question means we have not really departed the French coast—we have merely tried to hide behind a figment of 'contemporaneity'. The very identification of the globalisation narrative with the names of Baudrillard, Lyotard and Virilio means that we need to stand back from this too if we are seriously to consider the impact of recent French theory.

There are other routes to thinking about our picture of Paris besides the arguments in French theory itself. There are certainly less sophisticated approaches to Paris. Paris as a tourist location provides a popular parallel to its place in the academic calendar of intellectual exchange. The following is an extract from a newspaper supplement chosen at random from brochures on European travel. It introduces Paris as the centre of 'life':

> France has an aura unparalleled anywhere. It has an air of expectancy about it, a feeling that things are always happening, an atmosphere of amour and the buzz of life itself. Nowhere is it more apparent than in Paris, undoubtedly one of the great capitals of the world.

This is a typical description of Paris: a world capital unique for the intensity of 'life' which happens there. Paris appears as the point at which characters from English-speaking countries come to lose themselves in the hazards of romance and sensual pleasure. In Henry James' novel *The Ambassadors*, the American character Strether finds his normal order of existence unbalanced by the diversions of the Parisian streets. The stereotyped Anglo subject exists in a tightly ordered system of accountability, for which every action compels a reason. Paris appears as the location in which this obsessive hold can be loosened and the Anglo subject distracted by the 'life' spilling into its streets.

In case this picture of Paris appears specific to fictional discourse, a selection of excerpts from travel talk by young Australians demonstrates its penetration into everyday conversation:

> There was something, a different atmosphere in Paris. It was more alive and there everyone was doing things and going places, always busy and it was really alive.

> I loved Paris. When I got there, I don't know, it was just so unreal, to actually be in this very famous city, and my first response was to love it. To love seeing these things that I'd seen only in photographs before.

> Paris was the first continental place that we got to. And it was a bit frightening, cos it was so different. And it was the first place we'd been to which didn't have the English language as spoken by the majority. But after a day there, you could really let yourself sink into the Parisian life.[16]

No doubt Paris may be seen as one of the stops in a more general pilgrimage to the centres of history in Europe. But its particular status appears as a location which can distract a traveller from normal habits: you feel alive in Paris, France.

This sketch suggests a space for things French which writers such as Derrida might occupy within an English-speaking culture: that things French reveal phenomena which negate the practical order of sense—they can show how text defies meaning. This is by no means an unfamiliar position. In *Phaedrus*, Socrates argues that the souls of philosophers are closer to the world of ideal forms; in contrast to the 'common ambitions' of most people, philosophers are gripped with the 'madness' of lovers. Here there is room to think about the imaginative role of Paris as a site for philosophical truths that are at odds with the practical rationality of daily life. Such a space may free thought from the limiting question of what use it can be put to. This Paris may indeed be *romantic* in the sense that it distracts thought from the 'real world'.

To think about the 'usefulness' of recent French theory may thus be contrary to its tenor in our thinking—French theory inhabits a space in Anglo thought that is outside practical rationality. Paris is granted special exemption from the claims of usefulness that are normally employed to judge ideas. Should our inquiry therefore cease with the coda 'Ah, Paris, *vive la différence*'? But it is just beyond this point where there is thinking to be done. Why do we need this Paris? Perhaps Paris serves as a kind of utopia for alienated intellectuals. It is as true today as it was in the nineteenth century that the dominant values of English-speaking cultures concern productivity. For this reason, intellectual activity is marginalised: freedom from utility is one of the conditions of critical thought. As a utopic space, Paris provides an imagined location that is specially reserved for 'thinking'. This comment by John Tittensor provides an example of how Paris can be seen as an intellectual utopia:

> People [in Paris] are *interested* in writers, in why they choose their craft and how they exercise it and what they think about Life and Art and Politics and France and The World in General. There is no deference, deferring is not the French way; writers are seen as part of the fabric of society, as sources of ideas and necessary provokers of discussion; and discussion, of course, *is* the French way.[17]

Rather than have to defend their government grants against the resentment of the taxpayer, French intellectuals appear to be actively sought after as a significant voice in their own culture. For intellectuals in English-speaking countries, Paris is good for morale: it is a working example of how things could be otherwise.

It is this yearning for Paris among intellectuals which is the target of much satire concerning French theory. While this yearning may seem to lay the ground for change in English-speaking culture, it can also immobilise the intellectual into a form of 'dreaming': 'this Anglo world is too crass to bear thinking, it is better to be elsewhere'. In this light, then, Paris is used as a source of exotic fashions paraded by groups anxious to distinguish themselves from the multitude.

THEORY AS FASHION

Is there an element of truth in this satire? Could it be possible that an openness to the complex texts of Derrida is in part due to a sentimental residue for things Parisian—the same partiality which may exist for other cultural items, such as Chanel No. 5? Is this why Derrida is more popular in English-speaking universities than his own? These are perhaps the thoughts entertained by those more traditional thinkers who claim that recent French theory is simply a 'fashion', destined to pass once common sense is restored. I would claim that to dismiss this opinion as provincial philistinism is to follow the predictable pattern: isn't this 'turning up the nose' at popularisation just what is expected of intellectual snobs? I propose instead to give this idea all the rope it needs.

So the French are theoretical sophists, and their followers here cling to gleanings of Parisian *savoir faire* in order to distinguish themselves from the masses. Bradbury's satire makes the link between these ostentatious displays of knowledge and the conspicuous consumption of French goods:

> Like the finest French vintages—with which, it must be admitted, the leading participants are from time to time confused—the great names and the finest labels of the movement are spoken of everywhere, though as with the wines not all those who know the labels seem entirely aware of the contents of the bottles. Like the best French *couture*, the tags speak not only of quality but the highest *chic*, and are safe guarantees that one is getting not thought off the peg but the best possible design in the field of ratiocination.[18]

The import of this picture here is clear: those who follow French thought are more concerned with appearances than reality; they are a class of consumers rather than producers; they are victims of fashion rather than proponents of an alternative ideology; they need not be taken seriously.

This is perhaps what the label of 'fashion' does to an idea: those who profess it are seen as self-admiring victims and secondary to the main business of life. The German sociologist Georg Simmel puts this in the context of cultural imperialism in his 1904 essay on fashion:

> The currency, or more precisely the medium of exchange among primitive races, often consists of objects that are brought in from without. On the Solomon Islands, and at Ibo on the Niger, for example, there exists a regular industry for the manufacture of money from shells, etc., which are not employed as a medium of exchange in the place itself, but in neighbouring districts, to which they are exported. Paris modes are frequently created with the sole intention of setting a fashion elsewhere. Judging from the ugly and repugnant things that are sometimes in vogue, it would seem as though fashion were desirous of exhibiting its power by getting us to adopt the most atrocious things for its sake alone.[19]

From this global perspective, Simmel claims that Parisian fashion has an emulsifying effect on other countries: it separates off exotic pockets from the common standards. A French trend is adopted 'for its sake alone'.

This then, perhaps, is the anxiety grounding the label of 'fashion': that a currency exists which one cannot exchange with the official values of common sense. It performs no useful function. Perhaps I have cast this attitude too rigidly, but it is better to lay open such claims forcefully than let this divide persist unchallenged.

The idea of theory as fashion serves to dismiss post-structuralism as a short-lived movement, destined to change once the clique becomes bored, or its ideas become too accessible. It is no surprise, therefore, that narratives are emerging now about the 'death of French theory'. In a recent review of French academic life, Thomas Pavel[20] constructs a picture that limits post-structuralism to conditions that are specific to an 'ideological elite'. The connection between this elite and post-structural theory is made in two ways: as fashion and as frustrated imperialism. In terms of fashion, Paris has a highly concentrated intellectual life which demands a rapid turnover of ideas—what emerges is likely to be superseded within a generation. And in terms of imperialism, Pavel argues that post-structuralism was the product of the yearning in French intellectuals for empire: the dissolution of the French empire led to a transfer of allegiance to the Soviet bloc—allegations of totalitarianism are countered by the doubt cast by thinkers such as Foucault on the 'freedoms' of western liberalism. In the current scenario, a new generation of young Turks combined with the unavoidable recognition of the failure of the Soviet system have served to relegate the works of post-structuralism to second-hand Parisian bookshops. What has replaced it is a renewed faith in independent scholarly activity, in which history is seen as a function of individual action and local strategies. The semiotic empire departs along the same path on which it arrived: the catwalk of theory. In its place are the more sober schools of neo-historicism and structurationism which point to a host of micronarratives rather than epic (non)systems of philosophy. (This season's fashion is more individual and subdued.)

Well, should we feel liberated now this decadent regime of Parisian theory has crumbled? There are two points worth making here. First, much of the criticism of French theory as the expression of the conditions peculiar to Paris—as subject to fashion and imperialist ambitions—does not necessarily generalise to its uses in other cultures. It is difficult, for instance, to think of Australian intellectuals identifying with a lost empire. The picture of Paris as an intellectual hothouse perhaps reinforces the need for other communities to give the ideas that emerge there the time they need to take root and bear fruit. The second point concerns the alternative posed to post-structuralism. The return to an academic community in which scholars work within their own autonomous fields seems at first to guarantee a certain level of freedom and difference—not everyone has to study the function of signification. Yet the basic paradigm offered for this renders academic work homogeneous: you till your plot of land with exactly the same method as everyone else. The methods are all the same: find out what the goal is, and then interpret action as a strategy for its realisation. It is in this way that the post-structuralist movement has been explained as an act of imperial restoration: see the goal as the restitution of the French empire and interpret the linguistic turn of recent French thought as a means to this end.

There are two serious omissions in this paradigm. The first is the possibility of conversation across the minor specialisations: will a student of Renaissance English Court poetry have anything to say to someone researching African post-colonial politics without resorting to some general philosophy of meaning and power? We risk becoming bogged in a mode of interpretation by which all actions are seen simply as means to an end, and books are judged without reference to their covers. Second, we risk not being able to see outside the framework of practical rationality, where decisions are made on the basis of the most efficient means to pre-established ends. While this

value dominates the official stage—gearing the universities to production, the technologisation of sport, etc.—it leaves unspoken the
question of the end towards which this activity is directed. Without
a means of stepping outside practicalities, a culture threatens to close
in on itself. This is why an English-speaking culture must always turn
to more expressive cultures in order to frame moments of solidarity,
where some end is in sight—Malcolm Bradbury and friends will still
resort to champagne to mark a common achievement. The Anglo
reader's curse of 'fashion' disavows a lack in the capacity to reflect
on one's projects. And as such it leaves the ends that are already in
place unquestioned.[21]

In the argument about theory as fashion we are faced again with
the alternative pictures of Paris held by Llull and Valéry. In the
context of recent French theory, Paris acts as a 'lamp of truth' by
providing an *aperture* through which ideas that are counter to the
dominant interests can enter into conversation. And as 'bonfire', it
offers a *currency* for the expression of local interests whose circulation is restricted to a fashionable few. One picture takes a romantic
view of theory as a truth remote from everyday concerns, and the
other rests in a practical perspective where all actions are strategies
of power. The argument between these two perspectives is what
makes French theory a 'live event', responded to differently by different audiences. It is this response that might be called 'the judgment of Paris'.

THE JUDGMENT OF PARIS

The alternatives of power and truth represent a philosophical narrative that is reproduced not only in Plato's *Phaedrus*, but also in the
fable of Paris the god. In Greek myth, 'the judgment of Paris' refers
to the choice granted the god Paris between the offerings of three
goddesses. Helen, in Euripides' *Women of Troy*, tells the story:

> Paris was made judge between three goddesses. Athene's bribe was
> this: that he should lead the Phrygians to war and destroy Hellas.
> Hera promised him a throne bestriding Asia and Europe, if he
> placed her first. Aphrodite, with extravagant praise of my beauty,
> promised him that, if he judged her the loveliest, I should be his.
> What next? See how the story goes. Aphrodite won; and from my
> marriage Hellas gained this benefit: you today are neither
> overwhelmed by Asian armies, nor ruled by an Asian king. The
> gain for Hellas was for me disastrous loss ... [22]

The choice granted Paris is between the qualities of military
strength, political power, or beauty. This can be reduced to two

alternatives: power or truth. There is no purely rational way of making such a choice. Recent French theory presents all English-speaking cultures with a challenge: is there anything that exists without a reason which is not rubbish? The thinking from Paris is that reasons come later.

It may seem that this scenario is too lofty for local thinkers, particularly from a country that stands to the side of major-league intellectual life. Yet there are conditions peculiar to an Australian context which grant a freedom to think otherwise about ideas. The geographical and cultural distance from Paris inhibits many French writers from coming to universities and talking directly about their theories.[23] In order to disseminate their ideas, therefore, it often happens that local academics take a specialist interest in one particular writer, for whom they are sometimes called on to speak. Though mostly this voice clarifies the original texts and defends the perceived intentions of the absent writer, in the context of this volume the contributors have been given the licence to stand back from their authorised involvement, and speak to the relationship between their writers and foreign contexts in which they are read.

The essays have been divided into three groups according to the kinds of possibility drawn from the French author: writing, reading and social uses.

The first group of essays deals with the potential for writing uncovered by French theory. Kevin Hart reveals the space present in Derrida's work for contextualisation, or 'counter-signing' the text. Hart shows how he has used this space to work with poetic possibilities uncovered by the instability of meaning in language. Brenda Ludeman presents testimony to Kristeva's project of *semanalysis*: she claims that it serves to liberate a previously occluded materiality of meaning. This is something which Ludeman presents as a unique promise for an art writing that is not contained within the monologic narratives of academic art history. David Odell points to Blanchot's recovery of the forgotten moment in dialectical thinking: a consciousness in abeyance to the infinitely knowable, what Odell names the 'gnostic sublime'. Odell describes the form of *récits* employed by Blanchot as a means of having theory speak through fiction. In the case of Hart, Ludeman and Odell, French theory has been able to point towards an understanding that is lacking in the Anglo picture—that is, how language 'speaks'—and point as well to the possibilities this allows in the practice of writing.

One way of reading French theory is to use it as the measure of one's intelligence: how far can I as a reader reach towards the subtle consciousness contained in the texts? Other ways of reading French theory are presented by Virginia Trioli and Henry Krips. Trioli takes Barthes' view of the involvement of the reader in the text to develop a narrative about her own autobiographical relation to his writing. The far-reaching light Barthes sheds on the relation of reader to text is used to reflect the act of reading Barthes so that reading becomes writing and the distance between text and life almost cancelled. Krips traces the discursive space opened to the English-speaking reader by Foucault's *History of Sexuality*. Foucault is placed in the position of revealing the story that in many ways is the one that contemporary western readers live their lives by: as beings 'liberated' from repressions. Is Foucault then liberating his readers from this narrative? Krips demonstrates that Foucault's text fails to point to any single ethical response. This indeterminacy is seen to open the text to the effects of context. The readings of both Barthes and Foucault therefore point to the existence of fictions by which lives can be organised.

The final group of essays concerns itself with the social contexts in which the texts of particular French writers may be seen to operate. Peter Cotton's discussion of Lacan places his psychoanalysis between the technocratic attitude of the Anglo-American psychotherapeutic scene and the historical picture present in the works of Heidegger. Though Lacan provides an alternative to an attitude where effectiveness is prior to understanding, he is seen by Cotton to be unable to account for the historically specific nature of the split subject which he sees as a symptom of the modern principle of 'self-positing'. The political setting constructed for Baudrillard's texts by Chris McAuliffe concerns the particular struggle against orthodox Marxism whose reductivism he hoped to expose. McAuliffe contrasts this tactical use of Baudrillard with the 'radical loss' which Baudrillard is seen as promoting in his reception in the Anglo art world. Such an alternative makes reading Baudrillard a more active pursuit on behalf of the reader. Julian Pefanis' chapter on Lyotard presents a writer who has set himself up against both Freud and Marx. Pefanis shows some of the specific roles of Lyotard's text in informing an anti-militancy in Paris. Finally, Clare O'Farrell provides a 'double reading' of Bourdieu: she gives an account of his theory and then attempts to situate it within the social milieu of Paris. Cotton, McAuliffe, Pefanis and O'Farrell all actively read their authors to discover their place in the argument and place their ideas in a context of use rather than truth.

In general, the recent French theory spoken of in this volume gives space to the process of representation: not just the book, but its cover as well. This is a space denied by the reductive emphasis on practical rationality dominant in the Anglo mind. This kind of space extends into poetry, art, autobiography, politics, etc. Certainly the contributions point also to some shortcomings in the make-up of these theories, but this seems almost necessary to keep them open for dialogue with different cultures.

In order to highlight their response to French theory, some of the writers in this volume have taken chances with the standard academic voice. A reader might be advised to think of these as attempts to give life to ideas, rather than rehearse a series of ready-made points. If nothing else, these attempts should serve to lay open the space in which it becomes possible to 'own' one's allegiance or antagonism to Parisian ideas, to think that one might not be simply following a fashion from elsewhere. And maybe in doing this we can turn our backs on the bonfire, and see what of our own world comes alive in its glow.

NOTES

1 J.-J. Rousseau *Emile* transl. B. Foxley, London: J. M. Dent & Sons, 1911, p. 307

2 *English Traits* London: George Routledge & Sons, 1848

3 J.N.Hillgarth *Ramon Llull and Llullism in Fourteenth-Century France* Oxford: Clarendon Press, 1971, p. 151 (my emphasis); see also Anthony Bonner (ed.) *Selected Works of Ramon Llull* vols 1 & 2, New Jersey: Princeton University Press, 1985; for a more philosophical outline of Llullian thought, see Francis A. Yates *The Art of Memory* London: Routledge & Kegan Paul, 1966.

4 'Letter from a Friend' *Monsieur Teste* transl. J. Matthews, Princeton, NJ: Princeton University Press, 1973, pp. 50–51

5 'No Identity' *Collected Papers* transl. Alphonso Lingis, Dordrecht: Martinus Nijhoff, 1987, p. 147

6 Mikhail Bakhtin *Problems of Dostoevsky's Poetics* transl. Caryl Emerson, Manchester: University of Manchester Press, 1984, p. 88

7 ibid. p. 89

8 M. Bradbury *Mensonge* London: André Deutsch, 1987, p. 17

9 Bruno Latour *Science in Action* Milton Keynes: Open University Press, 1987

10 S. Weber *Institution and Interpretation* Minneapolis: University of Minnesota Press, 1987, p. 31

11 ibid. p. 41

12 *A World of Difference* Baltimore: Johns Hopkins University Press, 1987

13 Of course, there is a more angry form of impatience with the success of French theory. Jean-Michel Roy ('The French Invasion of American Art Criticism' *Journal of Art* 2, 2, 1989, pp. 20–21) complains of the uncritical acceptance by art critics of ideas attached to French proper names: ' . . . is language 'fascist' simply because Barthes said so?'.

14 The perspective of 'moral topography', in which different countries are seen to participate in an argument is elaborated further in K. D. Murray 'A life in the world in Australia' *Australian Cultural History* 10, 1991, pp. 32–45).

15 *English Traits* p. 141

16 This travel talk is part of a corpus of 80 hours of discussion about the experience of being overseas. It was collected as part of a doctoral thesis investigating how sense is made of personal change.

17 John Tittensor 'French books and writing' *Meanjin* 44, 1985, p. 535

18 *Mensonge* p.17

19 Georg Simmel 'Fashion' *American Journal of Sociology* 62, 1957, p. 545

20 Thomas Pavel 'The present debate: News from France' *Diacritics* 19, 1989, pp. 17—32

21 This picture grants a role to French thought which the Russian theorists Lotman and Uspensky (Y. Lotman and B. Uspensky 'Semiotics of culture' *New Literary History* 9, 1978, pp. 211–32) might term a 'de-automatising mechanism': a mode of presencing which counters the closed rationalities of accounting systems.

22 Transl. Philip Vellacott, lines 924–933

23 At a recent meeting hosted by the marxist journal *Arena*, a discussion about deconstruction and politics raised such conflicting representations of Derrida's ideas that it was suggested as a joke that he should be phoned and thus settle the issue with a definitive statement.

PART I
Writing

Kevin Hart's chapter on Derrida is a reflection on the poetic implications of theory. Hart seeks to explain several aspects of Derrida's writings by an analysis of his recent work on proper names and signatures. In the slippage between text and proper name, Hart sets out the space for local readings of deconstructive theory and uses his own poetic practice as a demonstration of this.

KEVIN HART

1   Jacques Derrida
'*The most improbable signature*'

Literary theory, as currently practised in the academy, answers to a familiar roll of names: Roland Barthes, Jean Baudrillard, Paul de Man, Jacques Derrida, Michel Foucault, Julia Kristeva, Jacques Lacan and Claude Lévi-Strauss. The list could easily be expanded, and almost any combination of names can be cashed out as a critical position that is more or less viable in the institution. But the chances are that one name would appear in the reading list of any group interested in criticism, regardless of its political commitment or disciplinary background: I mean 'Jacques Derrida'. Over the last decade or so, Derrida's name has appeared in a surprising number of different contexts.[1] I say surprising because, on the face of it, one would think his work is too dense and too allusive to become popular, even among academics. Odd though it is, Derrida has become a very popular figure. People interested in architecture, art, education, legal studies, literature, philosophy, politics, psychoanalysis, social theory and theology (and many other things besides), have been drawn to various aspects of his thought. One hears the name 'Jacques Derrida' in a pop song by Scritti Polliti; it is proclaimed on badges and T-shirts; and in France one can buy a cassette of him reading a recent text, *Feu la cendre*. Just why Derrida has attracted such attention, especially in America, would make a fascinating study. It would doubtless be a story of admiration and antagonism, discipleship and misrepresentation, and much in between. And it would surely include a chapter on his time at Yale. For while Derrida's name has been asterisked for special consideration in the Yale departments of English, French and Comparative Literature, elsewhere on the campus it has been given a black mark. Thus in

1984 Mrs Ruth Barcan Marcus, the Halleck Professor of Philosophy at Yale, wrote to the French Government protesting against Derrida's nomination to the position of Director of the International College of Philosophy:

> To establish an 'International College of Philosophy' under Derrida's charge is something of a joke or, more seriously, raises the question as to whether the Ministre d'Etat is the victim of an intellectual fraud. Most of those informed in philosophy and its interdisciplinary connections would agree with Foucault's description of Derrida as practicing 'obsurantisme terrioriste' [sic].[2]

Joker or terrorist? Neither description of Derrida is apt, yet one can see why someone like Ruth Barcan Marcus objects so strongly to him. One example should suffice. A good deal of Derrida's recent work has been on proper names and signatures, problems of the borderline. Not that an analytic philosopher should think badly of someone addressing such issues: nomination and reference, speech acts and translation, are perfectly respectable topics for research and teaching. Less respectable, though, is the way in which Derrida tackles these questions. It is partly a matter of strategy, partly a question of style. To take a rather extreme example, *Glas* is composed of two columns, one dedicated to Hegel and one to Genet. 'His name is so strange', writes Derrida of Hegel.

> From the eagle it draws imperial or historic power. Those who still pronounce his name like the French (there are some) are ludicrous only up to a certain point: the restitution (semantically infallible for those who have read him a little, but only a little) of magisterial coldness and imperturbable seriousness, the eagle caught in ice and frost, glass and gel.[3]

That the proper name 'Hegel' sounds like the French for eagle, *aigle*, is significant for Derrida though not, I would think, for Marcus.

For what interests Derrida is that 'Hegel' cannot be limited to its proper task of referring to the author of *The Phenomenology of Mind*, the *Science of Logic*, and so on, but gets involved in signifying patterns and catches improper significations from them. The border between reference and meaning is not impregnable: a point that Derrida states, demonstrates and uses as a means of composition. It is this last aspect of Derrida's writing, in which he styles himself a creative writer as much as a philosopher, that some people find intensely annoying and unprofessional. But Derrida is unrepentant, and the eagle keeps reappearing on both sides of *Glas*: for Hegel, as an image of Jewish and Christian spirituality, yet also when evoking

Hegel's admiration for Napoleon, 'the only eagle before which speculative idealism kneeled'; and for Genet as an image of the thief's freedom from the law: 'I shall gaze over the world with the clear regard that the eagle imparted to Ganymede'.[4] So Derrida is using Hegel's name as a means of writing *Glas*, coupling the philosopher of law with the homosexual novelist and thief to produce a 'bastard course'.[5]

The insistence that philosophy is written, that it can never present its object of enquiry, whether being or knowledge, is Derrida's main theme. In *Glas* this appears in remarks that follow the evocation of Hegel as an imperial eagle:

Who, him? The lead or gold, white or black eagle has not signed the text of *savoir absolu*, absolute knowledge. Even less has the red eagle. Besides, whether *Sa* is a text, has given rise to a text, whether it has been written or has written, caused writing, let writing come about is not yet known.

Sa from now on will be the siglum of *savoir absolu*. And *IC*, let's note this already since the two staffs represent each other, the Immaculate Conception. A properly singular tachygraphy: it is not first going to dislocate, as could be thought, a code, i.e., what we depend [*table*] on too much. But perhaps, much later and more slowly this time, to exhibit its borders

Whether it lets itself be assigned [*enseigner*], signed, ensigned is not yet known. Perhaps there is an incompatibility (rather than a dialectical contradiction) between the teaching and the signature, a schoolmaster and a signer. Perhaps, in any case, even when they let themselves be thought and signed, these two operations cannot overlap each other [*se recouper*].[6]

In a seminar dedicated to 'Otobiographies', an essay on Nietzsche, Derrida offers a useful gloss on this passage:

In *Glas*, I said that Hegel seemed not to sign; and yesterday I began by saying Nietzsche is someone who wanted to sign. That appears to be the case. Hegel presents himself as a philosopher or a thinker, someone who constantly tells you that his empirical signature—the signature of the individual named Hegel—is secondary. His signature, that is, pales in the face of the truth, which speaks through his mouth, which is produced in his text, which constructs the system it constructs. This system is the teleological outcome of all of Western experience, so that in the end Hegel, the individual, is nothing but an empirical shell which can fall away without subtracting from the truth or from the history of meaning. As a philosopher and as a teacher, he seems to be saying basically that not only is it possible for his signature and his proper name to disappear without a loss, to fall outside of the system, but that this is even necessary in his own system because it will prove the truth and the autonomy of that system. Thus, my exclusion from what I am saying—the exclusion of my signature from my text produced through me—is absolutely essential and necessary if my discourse is to be a philosophical, ontological one. It appears, then, that Hegel did not sign.[7]

Or as Nietzsche wrote, somewhat more caustically: 'The only thing of interest in a refuted system is the personal element. It alone is what is forever irrefutable'.[8]

A philosopher like Ruth Barcan Marcus or may not agree with these remarks on Hegel's and Nietzsche's signatures; she may or may not think that Hegel and Nietzsche are worth discussing in the first place; but Derrida's comments plainly fall within the orbit of what passes for philosophical discussion at a colloquium, and it is unlikely that they would stir her to write a letter of complaint to the Ministère d'Etat. The passage from *Glas*, however, might well raise her indignation. What is at issue here are not simply philosophical claims, but a strategy and a style that are judged inappropriate to philosophical writing.

'Do you consider *Glas* to be a work of philosophy or of poetry?' asks Richard Kearney of Derrida. The reply is characteristic:

It is neither philosophy nor poetry. It is in fact a reciprocal contamination of the one by the other, from which neither can emerge intact. This notion of contamination is, however, inadequate, for it is not simply a question of rendering both philosophy and poetry *impure*. One is trying to reach an additional or alternative dimension beyond philosophy and literature. In my project, philosophy and literature are two poles of an opposition and one cannot isolate one from the other or privilege one over the other. I consider that the limits of philosophy are also those of literature. In *Glas*, consequently, I try to compose a *writing* which would traverse, as rigorously as possible, both the philosophical and literary elements without being definable as either. Hence in *Glas* one finds classical philosophical analysis being juxtaposed with quasi-literary passages, each challenging, perverting and exposing the impurities and contradictions in their neighbour; and at some point the philosophical and literary trajectories cross each other and give rise to some *other* site.[9]

Hardly the work of a terrorist, this, and not really the work of a joker either. Yet if Derrida's overall concern is to show that philos-

JACQUES DERRIDA

ophy and literature are always already woven together, we can approach his work by following a single thread: his analysis of the proper name and the signature.

There are any number of places where we could begin. An interest in names is apparent in Derrida's earliest writings on Edmund Husserl, but the first sustained examination of the proper name occurs in his reading of 'A Writing Lesson', a chapter of Lévi-Strauss's *Tristes Tropiques*. Here the anthropologist relates his sojourn among the Nambikwara people, and of special interest are his remarks on the development of writing in their society. There is no mistaking Lévi-Strauss's fondness for the Nambikwara, for although he admits, at some level, that their society licenses violence, he prefers to affirm them as essentially uncorrupted and playful. Uncorrupted, that is, until the advent of writing, which aids the exploitation of mankind rather than its enlightenment. The French anthropologist introduces writing to the Nambikwara—with disastrous results: they immediately display all the classic signs of political intrigue, while knowledge becomes encrypted, private, the property of a hierarchy. 'Writing, on this its first appearance in their midst, had allied itself with falsehood.'[10] So writing, in this story, marks the fall of the Nambikwara from innocent nature to guilty culture.

At one point Lévi-Strauss confesses to a ruse he used to learn the names of the Nambikwara children. 'One day, when I was playing with a group of children, a little girl was struck by one of her comrades. She ran to me for protection and began to whisper something, a 'great secret', in my ear.'[11] The great secret is the name of her antagonist who, realising what has occurred, exacts revenge by telling the foreigner his informant's name. And so the story continues, each child entering a vicious circle of revenge, until the anthropologist knows all the children's names and, more, the adults' names. This incident interests Derrida because, as Lévi-Strauss tells us, the Nambikwara 'are not allowed . . . to use proper names'. A strict prohibition has been transgressed, and for Lévi-Strauss it is suggestive of the violence that disrupts an innocent people when their linguistic habits are contaminated by writing.

But has Lévi-Strauss really learned the proper names of all the members of the tribe? Derrida thinks not:

We know *a priori* that the 'proper names' whose interdiction and revelation Lévi-Strauss describes here are not proper names. The expression 'proper name' is improper, for the very reasons that *The Savage Mind* will recall. What the interdict is laid upon is the uttering of what *functions* as the proper name. And this function is

7

consciousness itself. The proper name in the colloquial sense, in the sense of consciousness, is . . . only a designation of appurtenance and a linguistico-social classification. The lifting of the interdict, the great game of denunciation and the great exhibition of the 'proper' . . . does not consist in revealing proper names, but in tearing the veil hiding a classification and an appurtenance, the inscription within a system of linguistico-social differences.[12]

Already part of a system of social classification, the proper names are not strictly proper. Each member of the tribe derives his or her apparent uniqueness and self-identity from a system of social differentiation that is in operation well before names are actually given.

In short, a name is *proper* only if it indicates a pure self-consciousness, an unsullied self-presence. We hear more of this in 'La Parole soufflée':

Proper is the name of the subject close to himself—who is what he is—and abject the name of the object, the work that has deviated from me. I have a proper name when I am proper . . . The unity of these significations, hidden beneath their apparent dispersion, the unity of the proper as the nonpollution of the subject absolutely close to himself, does not occur before the Latin era of philosophy (*proprius* is attached to proper) . . . [13]

What Derrida calls 'the metaphysics of the proper' operates, then, over a considerable field, involving all appeals to 'self-possession, propriety, property, cleanliness'.[14] To bring the proper into question is to pull a thread that runs through all Latin thought and is stitched into its dominant motifs: the individual subject as the ground of knowledge or morality; the idea of God as *causa sui*; the prizing of proper over figural meaning; the conception of labour as property; the sanctioning of private property as the mixing of labour with nature; the relations between patriarchy and property; and so on.

All those motifs can be shown, Derrida argues, not to originate in full presence but to derive from a play of differences and deferrals. That there is a strong desire for them to appear as self-present need not be stressed; the concepts of origin, identity and end are as deeply embedded in western culture as they are highly esteemed by its intellectual representatives. And here we come to Derrida's main methodological point: regardless of what it asserts, any text consists of differences and deferrals that subvert any possible recovery of a full presence. In some texts, however, the desire for presence is so strong that it conceals their structure, while the reader's desire for a reassuring presence is so powerful that the concealment is seldom

examined. Nonetheless, by a patient reading of the text, this concealment can be exposed, and the appeal to presence shown to depend
on a prior notion of difference. So presence is revealed to be a
construction, not a natural, universal or inevitable state of affairs,
and the demonstration that this is so is known as 'deconstruction'.

For Derrida, no name can be truly 'proper': the play of differences
that produces them also denies their appeal to self-presence. To
mount a case against the proper name is to argue against the presence of a unique being, whether a self-determining human subject or
a self-causing God. In saying this, though, it is important to clarify
just what is at issue. Derrida's quarry is not the subject; nor is it God
or religious belief. His target is metaphysics, understood as the science of presence, and his aim is to expose its limits. But there is a
difficulty, for the limits of metaphysics are not linear or indivisible; it
is impossible to recall metaphysics to its proper boundaries, to keep
it under strict surveillance. No discourse can be completely free of
metaphysics; it will inevitably help to structure any discussion of the
human subject or God. Even so, its work can always be detected in
a text, and, once discovered, it is always possible to rethink the
subject or God, to place them in a different configuration from the
one we have inherited in the long epoch from Plato to Sartre. It is
one thing to deny that the proper name refers to a singular, self-
present being, quite another to suppose that the proper name does
not have a function in a system. Committed to the first task, Derrida
is just as firmly persuaded that the second is neither possible nor
desirable.

So the 'proper name' does have a function, a power. Here is
Derrida trying to specify that power:

> At the moment of death the proper name remains; through it we
> can name, call, invoke, designate . . . death reveals the power of the
> name to the very extent that the name continues to name or to
> call what we call the bearer of the name, and who can no longer
> answer to or answer in and for his name. And since the possibility
> of this situation is revealed at death, we can infer that it does not
> wait for death, or that in *it* death does not wait for death. In
> calling or naming someone while he is alive, we know that his
> name can survive him and *already survives him*; the name begins
> during his life to get along without him, speaking and bearing his
> death each time it is pronounced in naming or calling, each time it
> is inscribed in a list, or a civil registry, or a signature.[15]

The name can be detached from its original context, including the
individual it purports to pick out, and used elsewhere. This becomes

vividly apparent at death when the name plainly survives its bearer, but it has always been true, throughout life, because it is a structural feature of all names. Or as Derrida goes on to say,

> death reveals that the proper name could always lend itself to repetition in the absence of its bearer, becoming thus a singular common noun, as common as the pronoun 'I', which effaces its singularity even as it designates it, which lets fall into the most common and generally available exteriority what nevertheless means the relation to itself of an interiority.[16]

There is, to be sure, a negative moment in Derrida's critique of the metaphysics of the proper. It would be hard not to sense what Hegel called 'the seriousness, the suffering, the patience, and the labour of the negative' in deconstruction;[17] yet it would be wrong not to acknowledge that deconstruction is also affirmative. The prefix 'de-' of 'deconstruction' has contributed too much to the overall sense of the word as it has been generally understood, and deconstruction may well come to be known as an affirmative rather than a negative style of reading. Certainly Derrida is happy for it to be known as 'affirmative interpretation'.[18] But how can a discourse that seeks to dismantle western metaphysics, that wishes to interrogate its most fundamental assumptions and leave no philosophical thesis properly in place—in what possible sense can deconstruction be called 'affirmative'?

If the negative labour of deconstruction concerns writing—it shows how the proper can never control and limit the energy of writing—its positive project is to do with reading. The tasks are closely related, and no continuous line can be drawn between them. For the sake of exposition, though, let the accent fall on reading, on affirmative interpretation. Deconstruction involves a rethinking of the history of western metaphysics; it marks that history by exposing the limits within which it operates, and exceeds it by showing that metaphysics cannot master those limits. These moments of excess are found in the exemplary texts of metaphysics, and it is precisely in reading these texts against the grain that its limits are made visible. Yet often Derrida does not read a text to put pressure on western metaphysics but rather to affirm those elements forgotten or repressed by the tradition. In other words, he does not stop at showing that a text overruns its limits, he explores the textual effects of that overflow.

All this can be seen in his discussion of the signature. Normally, one thinks of the signature's rightful place as outside the text where it serves to gather the text into a unity, to declare the existence of an authorial consciousness which was the text's source, to affirm the author's legal right over the text—in short, to control textual meaning. To sign a text, Derrida argues, is to declare oneself as an absent presence. As we have seen, this does not indicate merely a provisional absence, when one happens to be unable to stand beside the text, but a generalised absence, such as after one's death. For it is a structural trait of any sign or name, including the signature, that it can be repeated outside its original context, at any time and in any place. Or as Derrida boldly puts it, 'the "signature" event carries my death in that event'.[19] There is no authorial presence outside the text, signified by an appended proper name, which can absolutely control the text's play of meaning. The signature cannot remain outside the text, a sign of a present consciousness; it 'falls to the tomb', as Derrida says, leaving no firm ground for the operations of interpretation. An author's text is his or her crypt on which a proper name is emblazoned.

Not only is the signature a name written on a crypt, it also becomes a crypt itself. On the face of it, the signature marks the place where a living author once wrote—it is a tomb; yet it also forms a code, a crypt, inside the text. In a number of recent studies, Derrida traces a fall from an author's proper name outside the text to a common name inside the text. Thus in his study of the contemporary French writer Francis Ponge, *Signéponge*, Derrida identifies 'three modalities of signature'. First, we have 'the signature in the proper name . . . the act of someone not content to write his proper name (as if he were filling out an identity card), but engaged in authenticating (if possible) the fact that it is indeed he who writes'. Second, 'the set of idiomatic marks that a signer might leave by accident or intention in his product . . . We sometimes call this the style, the inimitable idiom of a writer, sculptor, painter, or orator'. And third, the 'general signature, or signature of the signature, the fold of the placement in abyss where . . . the work of writing designates, describes and inscribes itself as act, signs itself before the end by affording us the opportunity to read: I refer to myself, this is writing, I am a writing'.[20]

And so we see that certain texts signed 'Francis Ponge' have traces of his name inside them. There is a disconcerting slippage from nomination to signification such that the things evoked in the texts (a sponge, a Turkish towel, pumice-stone) reverberate with the poet's proper name (*éponge, serviette-éponge, ponce*). Ponge loses his proper name, it becomes a common name; yet there is a sense in which, through that very loss, he gains far more than he can ever lose. By deforming his proper name, letting it slip into lower case, Ponge

sends it out to occupy more territory. It begins to colonise the world
of things; while, at the same time, his proper name is monumen-
talised, writ large by the world of things.[21]

It is in writing in such a distinctive manner about ordinary things
such as meat, bread, an oyster, doors, and so forth, that Ponge
develops a characteristic idiom and style, and so signs his text from
within. And it is in foregrounding the materiality of language that
Ponge's text signs itself a third time, drawing attention to itself as
writing: as, for example, in 'L'huître' where a range of words with a
circumflex—*blanchâtre, opiniâtrement, verâdtre, noirâtre, aussitôt*—
suggests the oyster's shell.[22] Signature, thing and text: Ponge shows
us how each can become the other, how 'one can make of one's
signature a text, of one's text a thing, and, of the thing, one's
signature'.[23]

Unable to remain wholly outside the text, the writer's proper
name very improperly begins to act like any other signifier, allowing
Ponge's texts to be decoded along the lines of homonyms and ana-
grams of the poet's name. Derrida has a philosophical thesis to
propose, that no uninterrupted boundary can be drawn between
reference and meaning, but that point could be made in a few pages.
His time is taken up in showing as well as saying. He is attracted by
the ways in which textual accidents befall proper names, how signification overruns nomination, exceeding it without return. The positive import of Derrida's theory is that nothing can be overlooked
when interpreting a text; anything can be detached from its original
context, even a proper name, and inscribed within another context
where it becomes meaningful. Although the theory of the signature is
a discourse on being (the status of the author's presence and absence)
it is also a practice of reading, one that disrupts formalism and
historicism with equal force, and so opens the possibility of rethinking the relations between an author's life and writing.

In a world where the proper name cannot designate a unified
self-identical individual, and a signature cannot remain wholly outside the text, the question must be asked, 'Who signs?' And if we
must admit that nothing truly occurs in the present, that presence
never presents itself, we must also ask, 'When does a signature take
place?' The questions are closely related, but let us begin with the
first. There is no need to discuss pseudonyms, homonyms and such
things. They surely exist, but not everyone uses them, and the point
at issue is far more general. For no one is ever fully present to himself
or herself; there are always guises and ruses that one adopts, social
roles that must be played, and, indeed, are so habitual that, week by
week, one is barely conscious of them. Proust's Marcel portrays the

matter vividly when meditating on self-identity in *A la Recherche du Temps Perdu*: 'I was not one man only but the steady advance hour after hour of an army in close formation, in which there appeared, according to the moment, impassioned men, indifferent men, jealous men . . .'[24] So when I sign my name, it is both I and not I who signs.

Moreover, no signature can refer to a pure presence, a unique moment of signing; for, as we have seen, a signature is always already repeatable. At the moment when the pen touches paper, the signature is already a repetition of other signatures, including one's own, thereby making highly problematic the very words 'one's' and 'own'. Derrida expands on this theme with specific reference to Nietzsche:

> The signature becomes effective—performed and performing—not at the moment it apparently takes place, but only later, when ears will have managed to receive the message. In some way the signature will take place on the addressee's side, that is, on the side of him or her whose ear will be keen enough to hear my name, for example, or to understand my signature, that with which I sign . . . Nietzsche's signature does not take place when he writes. He says clearly that it will take place posthumously . . . when the other comes to sign with him, to join with him in alliance and, in order to do so, to hear and understand him . . . But it is not Nietzsche's originality that has put us in this situation. Every text answers to this structure. It is the structure of textuality in general. A text is signed only much later by the other. And this testamentary structure doesn't befall a text as if by accident, but constructs it. This is how a text always comes about.[25]

Every signature requires a countersignature; every signer needs someone to countersign for him or her, someone who listens carefully to what is written, and understands it, claims it for his or her own. In this sense, we are still helping Plato to sign his dialogues, and Shakespeare to sign his plays, when we read them closely, slowly, with care and understanding. It is precisely the signatures of writers as strong as Plato and Shakespeare that cannot be completed, in their time or ours.

The other comes to sign, then; yet signing is not without a risk, as Derrida explains in 'Télépathie':

> I do not make the hypothesis of a letter that would be the external occasion, in some way, of a meeting between two identifiable subjects—and which would be already determined. No, but of a letter which after the fact seems to have been cast toward some unknown recipient at the moment of its writing, a recipient

unknown to himself or to herself, if one can say that, and who determines himself or herself, as you know how to do so well, on receiving the letter; this is quite different from the transfer of a message. Its content and its end no longer precede it. Here's the point, you identify yourself and you organise your life on the programme of the letter, or rather of a post card, of a letter that's open, divisible, at once transparent and encrypted. The programme says nothing, it doesn't announce or state anything, not the slightest thing, it doesn't even present itself as a programme. One can't even say that it 'does' programme, as far as appearances go, yet without having the air of a programme, it *works*, it programmes. Then you say: it's I, uniquely I, who can receive this letter, not that it is reserved just for me, on the contrary, but I receive as a present the chance to which this card surrenders itself. It chooses me. And I choose that it should choose me by chance, I wish to cross its trajectory, I wish to find myself there, I can and I want to ... Others would conclude: a letter thus *finds* its recipient, man or woman. No, one cannot say that the recipient exists before the letter.[26]

A text can situate a reader in any number of ways: by means of grammar, rhetoric, tone, and selection of detail, one can be made to feel culturally intimate with a situation or quite the reverse. The various transactions that occur between text and reader can change from sentence to sentence, or even within a sentence. There are always new situations to negotiate in reading a text, and one scarcely registers them until one begins to read slowly and attentively. So the reader is always, to some extent, fashioned by what is read. It is as though the text says, 'If you want to read me, you'll have to obey my laws, move where I want you to move. Resist if you like, but too much resistance, or resistance of the wrong sort or at the wrong time, will prove useless to all concerned'.

All this is a commonplace of formalist analysis, but Derrida is making a slightly different, rather more eerie, point. A text's destination is irreducibly plural; no text, not even the most intimate love lyric, can be aimed at one reader in particular, excluding all others at all other times. Some texts are encountered by chance—you have a stroke of luck in coming across it at the right time. It touches you; the text matters; you have a stake in what it says, or how it speaks. It is as though the text pronounces your proper name, perhaps even a secret name; and in letting yourself be addressed, you appropriate the text, make it proper for yourself. The text does not tell you, in any definite sense, what you should be or how you should act; in fact, the fewer precise details about such things the better. Morally effective texts tend to be more successful the more they are underdetermined in terms of specific moral directions. After all, you can readily supply details from your experience, and it is your life that is to be changed, for good or ill.

There are people who have been utterly changed by reading a poem, a novel, an essay, or a philosophical treatise, at the right moment. St Augustine reading Paul's epistles in his garden in Milan one summer's day, and thence being converted to Christianity, is an extreme example; but each of us doubtless has similar, though less dramatic, stories to tell. (I sometimes think that my life as a poet has been programmed by reading Shelley's 'Ozymandias' in second form at school. It managed to turn a schoolboy who didn't like English into a writer.) Another kind of story, I suppose, concerns the sorts of changes that can happen—to the academy at large, to religious belief and political action, to teaching, reading, writing—in studying French theory here and now. At the very end of *Margins of Philosophy*, Derrida talks of 'the most improbable signature',[27] his own, and we may speculate a little on the destiny of that signature, posing the following questions: Who signs 'Jacques Derrida'? What makes that signature 'improbable'? Who countersigns his texts in Melbourne, Australia—to what ends, and with what effects?

The various games that Derrida plays with his proper name have received a good deal of attention.[28] There are many echoes of 'Jacques Derrida' in *Glas*, for example: 'D.J.' is overheard in *déjà* when discussing the way in which death inhabits the signature; when evoking the golden letters on his father's tomb, 'Derrida' becomes disseminated in *derrière le rideau*; and one can also read that name encrypted in 'Dionysus Erigone Eripetal Reseda'.[29] This legerdemain plays a thematic role in *Glas*—it continues the image of the 'Rembrandt torn into small, very regular squares' which begins the Genet column—as well as showing what is being said, that there is a continual circulation between proper and common names. If postmodern writers find this liberating and energising, it is unlikely to amuse a philosopher like Ruth Barcan Marcus. Nor, for that matter, will other things that Derrida does with his name. In *Writing and Difference* we find him signing one essay on Edmond Jabès's 'Reb Rida' and another 'Reb Derissa' which, taken together, spell 'Reb Derrida'; and Derrida has donned the mask, from time to time, of a Jewish rabbi.[30]

It would be naive to regard Derrida as pitting Jews against Greeks, yet there is a sense in which he does sign as a Jew. Hence this question regarding Parmenides, the father of Greek metaphysics: 'But will a non-Greek ever succeed in doing what a Greek in this case could not do, except by disguising himself as a Greek, by *speaking* Greek, by feigning to speak Greek in order to get near the king?'[31] The king here is the *archē*, the undemonstrable grounding moment of rational speculation, and Derrida's point is that philosophy has always laid claim to being the sole principle of intelligibility. To speak Greek, to be intelligible and rational, is to speak the language of philosophy. It has always been so. Yet what of the non-Greek, the Jew, the one who values the an-*archē*, the shifting ground of writing? There can be no direct discussion between Greek and Jew, philosophy and literature, because the debate is already structured in favour of the Greek. The only solution is to feign the language of philosophy, to use its privileged vocabulary but with bad intent: to bring the supremacy of its ground into question. In this way Derrida risks a theory that links the *archē* with the an-*archē*, that encompasses philosophy and literature in the one problematic.[32] Who signs 'Jacques Derrida'? There is no straightforward answer: he signs for literature and philosophy, it is true, yet also from a site (or, better, non-site) from which the two can be comprehended; and we must also remember that he signs in disguise. His is always an 'improbable signature'.

And that signature has a destiny in Australia. Derrida's writings have already been countersigned here: in the academy, the art world and the literary world. Perhaps too quickly, here as in America, for the name 'Jacques Derrida' has a way, even now, of dividing an intellectual community. There are those who regard the advent of French theory in Australia much as Lévi-Strauss considers the intrusion of writing among the Nambikwara, as something alien, disruptive, involving strange rites and secret codes. The myth of national innocence is still potent in Australia. And there is a kind of innocence, too, among Derrida's disciples: as though echoing his prose style and piously conserving his vocabulary could advance knowledge or literature. The spirit of deconstruction can almost be captured in the phrase 'thinking otherwise'. Derrida renders thinkable alternative ways of reading, writing, teaching, and so forth; and he does so by means of a subtle and pointed critique of the history of our dominant concepts. We can all learn from that critique, though we may not wish to import everything that he does with it. Derrida has liberated alternative ways of thinking; he has not legislated which ones to follow.

Which brings me to what I have learned from Derrida. To talk about the impact or influence of a writer on one's own work is never easy. If there were nothing else, there is always the difficulty of working out just what one has learned from someone, where it has

16

been applied, and with what success. I have been reading Derrida for the past ten years or so, and I suppose that aspects of his thinking and writing have helped to shape my own work in different ways and to different degrees. I could talk about how Derrida has influenced me in a number of areas—politics, religion, teaching, philosophy and literary criticism—but I want to be as specific and as practical as possible, and will therefore concentrate on what Derrida has meant to me in writing poetry. I started writing poetry at school, many years before I began reading Derrida; yet it would be fair enough to say that he has had a decisive influence on my writing. This could not have happened unless I also had an interest in *Of Grammatology*, *Dissemination*, *Glas*, and the rest, in their own right; and I only came across those books because I had been fascinated by other writers in the same 'tradition': a zigzagging tradition of argument and counterargument that encompasses Kant, Fichte, Hegel, Nietzsche, Husserl and Heidegger.

So I want to say something, by way of conclusion, about how Derrida has helped me write poems. I was drawn to his work because what he said about language seemed to ring true to my experience as a writer. And then I started to learn a great deal from him: not so much at the level of themes but in what he shows about structures, their curious patterns of revealing and concealing meanings. While I happen to admire several of Derrida's favourite writers—Blanchot, Celan, Jabès, Mallarmé and Ponge—I find his readings of those writers less useful than his commentaries on Plato, Hegel and Husserl. It is one thing to read Derrida as a model of how to write, as a doyen of postmodernism, and quite another to read him as a brilliant reader. Nothing could interest me less than trying to write like Derrida (or Bataille or Jabès or Sollers ...), but I find myself continually engaged and moved by the scrupulousness of his readings of dense philosophical texts. I find more there, for the writing of poetry, than in his style, although he is, in his way, a remarkable stylist of French prose.

This poem, 'Gypsophila', opens my fourth book, *Peniel*. It is, in its own way, a meditation on proper and improper names, though that was not its governing intention. As with all the poems I write, this one started with a phrase, a rhythm, an ambience that I half-sensed and wanted to evoke more completely, and not with anything that could reasonably be called an idea.

Another day with nothing to say for itself—
gypsophila on the table, a child's breath
when breath is all it has to name the world

and therefore has no world. It must be made:
her shadow sleeping on the wall, the rain
that pins fat clouds to earth all afternoon,

a river playing down the piano's scales.
This is the strangest of all possible worlds
with foam upon the beach, the sea's dead skin,

and lightning quietly resting in each eye.
Like gypsy camps or love, it must be made,
undone, then made again, like the chill rain

that falls without hope of climbing back,
content to leave its mark, for what it is,
upon the window or in the child's mind.

Gypsophila on the table, rain outside,
the child will tune the world to her desire
and make another world to keep in mind:

these breaths of air in which we softly wrap
the rain's glass stems to let them fall again
in sunlight, or flower for ever in the mind.

A world of things with nothing at all to say,
a margin that absorbs our silences:
the child must take the lightning from her eye

and place it in the sky, her shadow must
be told to fall asleep. This strangest world
in which we say *Gypsophila, Baby's breath*—[33]

I can hardly offer myself as a reliable guide to this lyric, but I will
say one or two things about how it came to be written. The image of
the margin is fairly direct evidence of having pondered over Derrida,
as is the queering of insides and outsides. More important for the
poem, though, is the way in which the name 'Gypsophila' is quietly
deformed into 'gypsy' and 'philia', one of the Greek words for love. If
I had not read *Glas* I would never have thought of breaking a word
into two false, etymological halves; still less would I have thought of
using it as a means of composing a poem. Yet I did compose the
poem in just that way: many of the images, and many of the moves,
derived from this one choice. I doubt that this odd combination of
technique and intuition would have affected anyone's reading of the
poem until this point. But now that I have mentioned this, it has
surely become significant. The borderlines between text and author,
between draft and finished product, have been divided.

One of the things that still surprises me about Derrida is the utter simplicity and power of his style of analysis. In reading a text, any text, he retraces its connection of ideas until he finds a gap in the argument; the text calls to be supplemented, yet it turns out that the gap cannot be adequately filled: the supplement always brings more than is necessary, supplanting what it supplies. A poem begins with more gaps than words, and in trying to complete it one is always trying to fill up those gaps. New material, even a single word, brings different significations into play, associations and connotations that reorganise everything that has gone before. In writing a poem, every image, every phrase, every word, is excessive. Critics may talk of formal unity, of balance and harmony, while the writer knows that a poem gains a semblance of poise only by suppressing its moments of excess. In breaking 'Gypsophila' into 'gypsy' and 'philia' I created a gap that had to be filled, and nothing I had learned from Derrida could help me fill it.

The proper name 'Jacques Derrida' does not appear in this poem, but I know (and now you know too) that, in a modest way, it countersigns his writings. And like any other text, it countersigns many other grand compositions: by Dante, Shelley, Montale and Bonnefoy, to begin with, not to mention Plato and Leibniz. None of these names raises the aesthetic value of the poem, yet, as I learned from Derrida, no text is ever free from philosophy or literature. We write in a complex tradition that, like it or not, writes us. This is not a matter of a cultural or cognitive cringe, only a recognition that European thought is at least as imperialist as European monarchs have been. Australia is marked by the 'white mythology'—the desire to be proper, to appropriate and expropriate—in more senses than one. But this leads us to other questions, and perhaps I have already said too much; as anyone knows who has read some Derrida, the last person to trust in reading a text is the one who wrote it:

> A text is not a text unless it hides from the first comer, from the first glance, the law of its composition and the rules of its game. A text remains, moreover, forever imperceptible. Its law and its rules are not, however, harboured in the inaccessibility of a secret; it is simply that they can never be booked, in the *present,* into anything that could rigorously be called a perception.[34]

NOTES

1 Good starting places for coming to terms with Derrida's writing are provided by Richard Kearney's interview with Derrida, 'Deconstruction and the Other' in R. Kearney (ed.) *Dialogues with Contemporary Continental Thinkers: The Phenomenological Heritage* Manchester: Manchester University Press, 1984, and Derrida's text, 'Letter to a Japanese Friend' in David Wood and Robert Bernasconi (eds) *Derrida and Différance* Warwick: Parousia Press, 1985.

2 J. Derrida *Limited Inc* Evanston, Il.: Northwestern University Press, 1988, 158 n.12

3 J. Derrida *Glas* transl. John P. Leavey, Jr and Richard Rand, Lincoln: University of Nebraska Press, 1986, 1a. In giving page references to this text, I follow the convention used in *Glassary* by John P. Leavey, Jr, Lincoln: University of Nebraska Press, 1986: *a* indicates the left column, *b* indicates the right column, and *i* indicates the insert.

4 *Glas* 184 ai, 57bi

5 *Glas* 6a

6 *Glas* 1a

7 J. Derrida *The Ear of the Other: Otobiography, Transference, Translation* ed. Christie V. McDonald, transl. Peggy Kamuf, New York: Schocken Books, 1985, p. 56

8 Friedrich Nietzsche *Philosophy in the Tragic Age of the Greeks* transl. Marianne Cowan, South Bend, Ind.: Gateway Editions, 1962, p. 25

9 J. Derrida 'Deconstruction and the Other' in Kearney *Dialogues* p. 122

10 Derrida quotes these lines as one of the epigraphs to *Of Grammatology* transl. Gayatri Chakravorty Spivak, Baltimore: Johns Hopkins University Press, 1976, Part II Section 1.

11 *Of Grammatology* p.111

12 ibid.

13 J. Derrida *Writing and Difference* transl. Alan Bass, London: Routledge & Kegan Paul, 1978, p. 183

14 *Of Grammatology* p. 26

15 J. Derrida *Mémoires: for Paul de Man* transl. Cecile Lindsay, Jonathan Culler and Eduardo Cadava, New York: Columbia University Press, 1986, pp. 48–49

16 *Mémoires* p. 50

17 G. W. F. Hegel *The Phenomenology of Mind* transl. J. B. Baillie, New York: Harper & Row, 1967, p. 81

18 J. Derrida *Spurs: Nietzsche's Styles/Éperons: Les styles de Nietzsche* transl. Barbara Harlow, Chicago: University of Chicago Press, 1978, p. 37

19 *Glas* p. 19b

20 J. Derrida *Signéponge/Signsponge* transl. Richard Rand, New York: Columbia University Press, 1984, pp. 53–54

21 Derrida goes so far as to claim that the transformation of one's proper name 'into things, into the name of things' is nothing less than the 'great stake of literary discourse' (*Glas*, 5b).

22 Francis Ponge *Le parti pris des choses: suivi de Proêmes* Paris: Gallimard, 1975, p. 43

23 *Signéponge/Signsponge* p. 20
24 Marcel Proust *The Sweet Cheat Gone* transl. C. K. Scott Moncrieff, New York: Vintage Books, 1970, p. 54
25 *The Ear of the Other* p. 51
26 J. Derrida *Psyché: Inventions de l'Autre* Paris: Galilée, 1987, p. 240; my translation
27 J. Derrida *Margins of Philosophy* transl. Alan Bass, Chicago: University of Chicago Press, 1982, p. 330
28 See, for example, Gregory L. Ulmer's *Applied Grammatology: Post(e)-Pedagogy from Jacques Derrida to Joseph Beuys* Baltimore: Johns Hopkins University Press, 1985, ch. 5.
29 *Glas* 19b, 68b, 112b. Geoffrey Hartman offers an illuminating analysis of 'Dionysus Erigone Eripetal Reseda' in his *Saving the Text: Literature/Derrida/Philosophy* Baltimore: Johns Hopkins University Press, 1981, p. 94.
30 *Writing and Difference* p.78, p.300. For a detailed discussion of Derrida's 'rabbinic' influences see Susan A. Handelman *The Slayers of Moses: The Emergence of Rabbinic Interpretation in Modern Literary Theory* Albany, NY: State University of New York Press, 1982, ch. 7. Derrida makes some observations on his Jewish background in an interview for *Le Monde* with Christian Descamps. See *Entretiens avec 'Le Monde': 1. Philosophies* Paris: Éditions La Découverte et Le Monde, 1984.
31 *Writing and Difference* p. 89
32 For a more detailed discussion of this point, see my *The Trespass of the Sign: Deconstruction, Theology and Philosophy* Cambridge University Press, 1989, ch. 4.
33 Kevin Hart *Peniel* Melbourne: Golvan Arts Press, 1991
34 J. Derrida *Dissemination* transl. Barbara Johnson, London: The Athlone Press, 1981, p. 63

Brenda Ludeman presents Kristeva's opposition between the semiotic and symbolic functions of language and points to the place of art in exposing the 'scission', or moment of instability that exists in the exchange between the two domains. This is a scheme she has applied in her art criticism (see 'The Monochrone paintings of Stephen Bush' *Art & Text* 31, 1989, pp. 73–75, in which she points to the conflict between the highly figurative nature of the works and the opacity of their rendering) as well as her own art practice (printing text on gallery walls, for example, *Proposals*, George Paton Gallery, University of Melbourne, 1988). In this chapter, Ludeman sets out the theoretical framework that she has developed from Kristeva's writing and put to use in her art criticism.

2 Julia Kristeva
The other of language

> ... to work on language, to labour in the materiality of that which society regards as a means of contact and understanding, isn't that at one stroke to declare oneself a stranger to language?
>
> Julia Kristeva[1]

In my initial encounter with the work of Julia Kristeva I happened upon the English translation of the text entitled *Desire in Language* and began to read and to reread several of the essays.[2] What I was receptive to in the writing was the allowance made for the textual and palpable status of language—a physical presence given as o t h e r to signification. Was it beneath the surface of language, or was it indissolubly the surface itself? How was it possible to make such a theoretical avowal of language as a site of exchange, of proliferation, of contiguity and of impulsion; of an expanding indifference to established meaning? As though desire listened to itself with an extraordinary theoretical and syntactical rigour. As though one heard what had been silent.

Or merely estranged, as in the essay 'The Father, Love and Banishment', which spoke of the paternal function and the conflictive relation between the subject, desire and meaning.[3] The categories of sexuality and desire were avowed here as a context for the analytical procedure, as a means of resistance to, and differentiation from, a symbolic use of language which would be permanently fixed, oriented towards death and the father. In this text Kristeva's speculation on the notion of a *paternity of death* aligned *permanence* with that which would be fixed (in effect a desire for ownership and thus the certainty of an immutable narrative space), for 'as long as a son

23

pursues meaning in a story or through narratives, even if it eludes him, as long as he persists in his search he narrates in the name of death for the father's corpses, that is for you, his readers'.[4]

According to Kristeva's account, to continue to narrate the story of such a paternity (which can only ever be, and nothing more than, the privileging of an order of sense in which meaning becomes permanent) is to remain transfixed by the primacy of the paternal. As the primary site of meaning, the space of death has been abrogated by the paternal through the use of linguistic constraints and classic narrative form. It is through the convention of an original unity which is disrupted and restored that the Other, feminised or woman, is repeatedly apprehended as a primary corpse, already dead, 'inert' to any meaning except that which is reiterated as consubstantial with the Law of the Father. The effect of this, as has been noted by Josette Feral, is to 'displace onto the feminine the full weight of the difference of the sexes, the full weight of lack, of death'.[5]

Paternity is thus established as that which is told or narrated as a defence against material discontinuity, as a continual deflection of that which is vulnerable and liable to material disintegration; a repeated disavowal or rejection of *matter*—of the *semiosis* of that verifiable mortality. One might relive here the inaugural moment, the triad of Father–Son–Death, were it not that one were as much a daughter as he himself had been, leading to exile, or. . .

> Banishment; an attempt at separating oneself from the august and placid expanses where the father's sublime Death, and thus *Meaning*, merges with the son's 'self' (but where a daughter can very easily become trapped) mummified, petrified, exhausted, 'more dead than alive'; a banishment robbing this sensible but always already dead, filial self of its silence on the threshold of a rimy minerality, where the only opportunity is to become anyone at all, and moreover, without the means for fading away. So flee this permanence of meaning. Live somewhere else, but in the company of paternal Death.[6]

And how is it that one might 'flee' this permanent order which privileges the Cartesian subject of discourse? At the conclusion of the essay 'The Father, Love and Banishment' (between the literature of Samuel Beckett and the painting of Giovanni Bellini, between death and exile) Julia Kristeva proposes:

> an other—untouched and fully seductive? The true guarantee of the last myth of modern times, the myth of the feminine—hardly

the third person any longer, but, both beyond and within, more and less than meaning: rhythm, tone, colour, and joy, within, through and across the word?[7]

Present in this writing and other essays in the volume is an *intertextuality*, known as 'the transposition of one or more systems of signs into another, accompanied by a new articulation of the enunciative and denotative positions'.[8] This intertextuality had two functions: to reveal what is banished in the act of predication and to account for the *intra-theoretical* discourses which comprise the epistemological sphere within which such a discourse is located.[9] Kristeva makes use of the term intra-theoretical to refer to that conjunction of disciplines which takes in psychoanalysis, linguistics, philosophy, and marxist discourse, in its role as an articulation of that desire for, and impulsion toward language itself, that is, toward the *materiality of language*. Kristeva's writing spoke that which previously could not be spoken, itself exiled, occluded, disavowed; it was a writing which spoke of the diverse materiality of language revealed through the elaboration of the notion of the *semiotic*.

For my own writing—in, through, and between the visual arts (a project essentially concerned with an investigation into a textual practice which sought to locate, appropriate, or speak from, the gap between literature and art practice)—the work of Julia Kristeva is seminal. The semiotic approach to writing was, and continues to be, enabling, in that it is receptive to the o t h e r of language, to that which had formerly been estranged, to the desire of the speaking and listening body, and hence to the possibility, rather than the privilege, of meaning. What was required for this *writing as textual space* was a theoretical account of the relations between textual practice and subjectivity. In Kristevan semiotics the particular method of analysis known as *analytical semiology*, or a semiotic analysis of writing and art practice, accounts for the position of the subject in textual practice, combining as it does the fields of linguistics, philosophy, and psychoanalysis. This analytical practice in turn rests on the materiality, or 'material order',[10] of language, which is to be found in that enabling modality, the propositional facility of the semiotic.

In the Kristevan thesis the diverse and material bio-psychical operation of the drives (heterogeneity) are seen to be the basis of that (negativity) which may dissolve, irrupt into, transgress or restructure any symbolic code. Heterogeneity, the movement of the drives or 'scission', is the basis for the essentially conflictive status of the signifying process, hence Kristeva's constant reference to the notion of a rending and renewing of social codes. The concept is a materialist reading of the Hegelian dialectical method. The negativity or productive dissolving, the drive which is referred to as a 'causality' in Kristeva's texts, which underlies all rational production and is capable of irrupting into the symbolic, is fundamentally heterogeneous, that is, it has a materiality.

The notion of a materiality of language, 'where the word is never uniquely the sign', owes much to accounts of poetic language such as are to be found in the work of the Russian formalists.[11] It should, however, be noted that this gesture towards a thesis of contiguity, as it is employed here, constitutes a differentiation in emphasis, or rather an elaboration of that which is articulated as pleasure and threat, the notion of heterogeneity, in Kristeva's texts.

As a textual practice, which locates itself in the place occupied by the *split subject* (the space from which one writes), analysis, and hence writing, requires a thesis of subjectivity. It is through Kristeva's complex and differentiated theoretical exegesis of the *subject* as the 'locus of textual production and deformation'[12] that the notion of *subjectivity* was, and continues to be, restored as a context for textual analysis.

The Kristevan thesis of the *semiotic* and the *symbolic*, as it is articulated in the texts *Revolution in Poetic Language* and *Desire in Language*, established a new relation between writing and art practice in which semiotics became the point of mediation. For Kristeva the function of art, or artistic practice, is to recognise that recursive moment in which *semiotic matter* splits and renews, and in so doing transforms the social code.[13] This process of production and differentiation is described variously as a movement, *scission*, or *productive dissolving* whereby

> the most radical heterogeneity . . . is maintained as the struggle against the signifier . . . but is at the same time, the site of the subtlest signifying differentiation. The former, which maintains rejection, takes us to the heart of jouissance and death; the latter—through subtle differences in rhythm or colour, or differences made vocal or semantic in laughter and wordplay— keeps us on the surface of pleasure in a subtle and minute tension.[14]

It is the premise of this paper that language itself, as *heterogeneous* matter, is the analogue for such a receptive process.[15] The notion of a materiality of language as a site of diversity which passes in and through the subject, is examined here in terms of a recognition that the symbolic function is that which would be fixed rather than that which is fixed.[16] The function of the symbolic order is to reproduce itself, recursively, and this results in the positing of representations which would appear to be fixed. However, this is no more than the action of that which would be fixed, for the symbolic is, as Kristeva notes, 'unstable', necessarily so, since it is this very instability which allows for a restructuring of meaning such as art practice. Materiality of language is examined as a speculation upon a form of discursive space—as a non-binary *elliptical* structure, or gap, inherent in language where it appears as an expanding indifference to meaning—which allows for the o t h e r of language to appear.[17]

A CRY FROM THE OTHER PLACE

What does it require then, the act of enunciation, the practice of art, of writing, the accession to discourse? An undeniably avowed position open to negotiation, open to that which is transgressive and speculative? Of what use may it be, and to whom, to acquiesce in an order of sense-making, to adhere to the strictures of the lexical and the syntactic, to affirm the status of all that had gone before? And what possible use can this be—this refusal to be explicit, to complete?

The pronoun *she* speaks of the indelible surface of the word, upsurge of language, over which signification proceeds; of an unassimilated cry, a refusal to omit, or to be complicit in the occlusion of the material status of language. The corporeal surface of the word, discernible as matter, as a tonality, as sound and as silence, is 'sustentation'. The notion of a carnal and sensate touch as metaphor for describing a particular relation to, and apprehension of, the other and of phenomena is to be found in the work of Emmanuel Lévinas and Luce Irigaray.[18] To apprehend this materiality is to be receptive to the other than visible, to the notion of a sensate inscription, which nevertheless remains indifferent, even hostile, to the lexical.

An *elliptical* space appears in signification, within the constraints of syntax, a space which may be apprehended aurally and textually, a space in which the visual can no longer maintain itself like an indissoluble narration. This gap or ellipsis, emerging like a stain, constitutes a refusal, capable of withstanding the occlusion exerted upon it by the proliferation of monological theses: a refusal in which the space of the material word extends into a carnal proximity with the other and thus becomes a not yet impossible structure.

It is in the aural and textual vicissitudes of language, an expanding material indifference, which is apprehended and transposed by the contiguity of the senses, that the dominant discourse, a sense order predicated on the historically privileged visual, founders. What this cry from the other place requires in the accession to discourse is an avowal of the material and the corporeal, as contiguous to, as that which is in proximity with the visual, rather than as a binary absence constructed in relation to the monology of a dominant sense.

In that dissolute moment which impels us toward enunciation and utterance, the palpable and yet absent o t h e r of language, which is language and yet which escapes from it, forms the matrix of an ever present pleasure and difficulty. When the word, the physical impulsion of language, is experienced with a cognisance of its palpability, then the materiality of language, of that which sustains and supports the subject, can no longer be disavowed.

THE MATERIALITY OF LANGUAGE

The Kristevan notion of the semiotic recognises and accounts for the corporeal dimension of any articulation, be it that of speech, writing or a mode of cultural production such as art practice. That is, the modality of the semiotic accounts for the appearance of the bio-physiological and the psychical in the linguistic process and in so doing accords a corporeality to those categories which were formerly described in terms of either the 'unconscious' (Freud) or that which was 'unrepresentable' (from the view of a discourse of transcendence which sought to flee the materiality of the lived body and was therefore predisposed not to recognise the imprint of such a physicality as it appears in language).

Nevertheless, the use and apprehension of language as matter, as that which pertains to a presence not reducible to the sign or to denotation, that is, as the presence of a palpable acuity, a bodily pulsion or rhythm, is to be found in contemporary accounts of the notion of poetic language. In Julia Kristeva's metalinguistic articulation of the signifying process, entitled *Revolution in Poetic Language*, the material status of language is avowed as an enabling modality which allows for the possibility and the dissolution of meaning. As Leon Roudiez notes, poetic language refers to the innumerable possibilities of all language practices, and 'all other language uses are merely partial realisations of the possibilities inherent in poetic language'.[19] The analysis of a language such as that referred to as 'poetic language' determines discursive space as speculative and propositional; it appears as a gap in, or struggle against, established symbolic structure, in order to 'challenge the closure of meaning'.[20] Throughout this text, and in other works by Julia Kristeva, such a permanence, or closure, is spoken of as a death, or more properly as murder. For Kristeva, 'Murder, death, and unchanging society represent precisely the inability to hear and understand the signifier as such—as ciphering, as rhythm, as a presence that precedes the signification of object or emotion'.[21] To deal in explication, in the name of death, of irony, of the parodic, of that which is unchanging, is then to ask of the text, or art practice, that it maintain itself like an indissoluble narration. In emphasising the presence and productivity of the *semiotic* (material processes) this account resists that which maintains the *symbolic* function of language, that is the privileged order of sense, the primacy of the visual (while recognising that all articulation takes place through the intersection of the two modalities), in order that a new textual space might appear. This site of exchange and proliferation appears, in, between, and through the dialectic of the semiotic/symbolic and moves toward the destruction of the boundaries between genres of cultural production which would sever and thus separate the poetic from the materiality of all language practice. In this order of sense (for which Kristeva's thesis provides a model) signification is not reducible to syntactic structure or a hierarchic order of sense; rather it is constituted as a complex operation which allows for the heterogeneous processes which impel the subject toward space and ultimately speech.

What is proposed here is that the accession to discourse may be maintained by an unhierarchic sense order in which all senses are merely *contiguous* to each other; it recognises that the arrival of meaning, the 'thetic' moment, requires both a recognition of established order (the symbolic and in particular the linguistic structure), and a differentiation from it (through an awareness of the presence, and passage, of that which may be apprehended through the contiguity of the senses, that is, an awareness of semiotic matter, for which the materiality of language becomes an analogue), in ways other than the either/or of sexual difference as it is posited by a binary modality. An avowal of the semiotic disposition and hence of the materiality of language, made viable through elliptical (nonbinary) structure, allows for the thesis of such a *contiguity*. Materiality may come to, and indeed does, signify, despite the constraints of linguistic structures, and it is therefore possible to accede signification to that which is, at the same time, occluded or anterior, since the thetic moment maintains the symbolic only as a privileged meaning, while the other, absent meanings, the *possibilities* of meaning, yet remain contiguous to the particular and privileged sense.

However, the materiality of language is (in relation to symbolic discourse) apprehended in the category of absence since it has been occluded, as that which is linguistically and carnally out of place, that which has been disavowed by the dominant sense order as an absent term in the field of signification. As a purportedly abstract and inaccessible realm, the place of the corporeal, the seen-to-be-absent, is in effect merely repudiated or disclaimed by the binary mechanism; having been elided in discourse, materiality exists in speech and in texts as *other*, as an alterity of language. It is this to which Kristeva refers in the following statement: 'I shall then be talking about something other than language—a practice for which any particular language is the margin'.[22]

The multiple, elliptical or occluded sites in which the o t h e r of meaning may be apprehended form the basis of a strategy or structure in which a viable discourse of the split subject may, and indeed does, function. *Elliptical structures* (hollow, vacancy, omission, gap) in language are non-binary, contiguous and regenerative. They constitute a forgetting, suppression or parturition of the codes of linguistic and social constraint. In Kristeva's texts this elliptical space as structure might be apprehended at that moment described as the 'apex of archaic, oneric, nocturnal, or corporeal concreteness, (which may, at the same time, account for) that point where meaning has not yet appeared (the child), no longer is (the insane person), or else functions as a restructuring (writing, art).'[23]

SEMANALYSIS

How then does Kristevan semanalysis, as a method for the analysis of art practices, account for the position of the subject in textual practice, and what is its relation to semiotics?

The project of semanalysis, as it is articulated in the work of Kristeva, directs the program of analysis toward the materiality of language and the discourse of the psychoanalytic subject. In the encounter with the particular art practice this mode of analysis is then able to account for that profound extremity, the propitiate unfolding of subjectivity, and for the work as a mediation of that process. For it is in the tenuous mediation between the lived body of the subject and the extant history which pre-exists that subject that one may apprehend the impulsion that sustains such a subjectivity, a process which has a material and a signifying function,[24] in the never complete production of the subject split between physical and psychical motivations. The discipline of psychoanalysis provides a context for the discussion of the semiotic motivations, which operate in and through language and art practice, and this in turn enables us to question and analyse the role of the libidinal economy in relation to cultural production. The need to account for the product, and the processes of its production, raises the issue of *exchange* not only between disciplines such as art history and cultural theory, but also between writing and art practice. What this allows for is a 'writing' which moves between categories or genres of cultural production in such a way as to bring into question the strict demarcations made between the visual, auditive and linguistic forms of that production, and to re-establish a relation of exchange between those categories.

Semanalysis then is an analytical method which locates and apprehends the semiotic disposition (that disposition which provides the material basis for signification, referred to as bodily rhythms or processes which are the precondition for speech and the accompanying material ground for all future signification) for the implications and traces of that disposition and of its material diversity, as it occurs in conflict with social constraints, in any given signification or art practice. In Kristeva's terms this disposition takes the form of a 'distinctive mark, trace, [or] index, the premonitory sign, the proof, engraved mark, imprint'.[25] Art practice is examined as the effect (of that mark or imprint) in the exchange or conflict which occurs in the interaction between the semiotic disposition and the symbolic (social constraints) in the process of signification.[26]

In the introduction to the text *Desire in Language*, Leon Roudiez notes that the etymology of analysis comes out of the Greek word *analyein*, to dissolve, referring to that action where the sign is dissolved or taken apart in order to open up new areas of signification. When taken in conjunction with a semiosis (the presence of 'instinctual drives as they affect language and its practice in dialectical conflict with the symbolic'),[27] analysis appears in that form described by Kristeva as the instance of a 'graft': as an analysis grafted onto semiology.[28]

In her preface to *Desire in Language* Kristeva speculates on the relation between psychoanalysis and the analysis of art practices: 'Grafted on to semiology, analysis here is not restricted to themes or phantasms; rather it scrutinises the most subtle, the most deeply buried logic of those unities and ultimate relations that weave an identity for subject, or sign, or sentence'.[29] Semanalysis is a means of analysing how meaning is produced and therefore it is the semiotic thesis of signification which in turn forms the basis of the analytical model; that is, the acquisition and practice of language, in the first instance, becomes a model for speaking about any given signifying practice. According to Kristeva's own definition: 'Semanalysis ... meets that requirement to describe the signifying phenomenon, or the signifying phenomena, while analysing, criticising, and dissolving "phenomenon", "meaning", and "signifier" '.[30] What occurs is a process whereby the presence of the semiotic is critically apprehended, and analysed, in its relation to the symbolic function in order to provoke an explication of the mediation of, and implications for, any given system of meaning.[31] Kristeva argues that given our status as split subjects, resting on the intersection of the rational and the irrational, semanalysis provides us with a means of acknowledging our ability to access structures of meaning (rationality) while dissolving those very structures in any given practice; in short, it accounts for the discourse of that subject.

In order to be able to articulate and apprehend the terms of such an encounter, on that escarpment, at the extreme edge of the other's flesh, the analyst (as subject) must also account for her/his own position in that discourse[32]—hence the procedure is 'doubly analytical'. For Kristeva it is this which makes the practice of semanalysis an ethical one, since in its attempt to analyse the production of meaning the subject/analyst maintains a necessary cognisance of the passage through such a process.[33]

THE INSTRUMENTS OF AN ANALYTICAL SEMIOLOGY

Julia Kristeva identifies the two modes necessary to the analytical project as 'radical instrumentalities'.[34] The first is that if meaning and its structures are to be questioned, it needs must be through reference to the condition of the subject as a speaking being.[35] The subject under question is the subject of psychoanalysis, the subject split between unconscious/conscious processes or motivations. Kristeva accounts for the discourse of this subject in the notion of the 'brink', which serves as a metaphor for a theoretical position which may hear and account for the other of discourse, the instance of a split, while bearing testimony to the sense of such a subjectivity.[36] The second instrumentality is the specific object of the analysis, that is, the practice of art (or literature).[37]

In the first place this gesture inserts the notion of subjectivity into the intra-theoretical sphere and in so doing confronts theories of signification (linguistics and philosophy) with the implications of the discourse of such a split subject.[38] In the second place, the practice of art becomes the privileged site of analysis and of dissolution, in accordance with Kristeva's view that it is in this practice whereby 'the dynamic of drive charges, bursts, pierces, deforms, reforms, and transforms the boundaries that the subject and society set for themselves' and further that to apprehend this practice 'we must therefore break through the sign, dissolve, and analyse it in a semanalysis, tearing the veil of representation to find the material signifying process'.[39]

Semanalysis recognises three basic principles which have been described by Kristeva as an implicit 'triple thesis' upon which the new status of writing, as an epistemological event, rests. The following statement lays out the thesis as it is given in the essay entitled 'How Does One Speak To Literature?'[40]

1 the materiality of writing (objective practice within language) insists on confronting the sciences of language (linguistics, logic, semiotics), but also on differentiation in relation to them;
2 its immersion in history entails the taking into account of social and historical conditions;
3 its sexual overdetermination orients it toward psychoanalysis, and through it toward the set of a corporeal, physical, and substantial 'order'.[41]

In terms of the first it can be seen that a writing which insists on an avowal of the material diversity of language, a cognisance of the semiotic disposition as facility, does conflict with, or is subversive of, symbolic language (as a linguistic code which rests on a privileged order of sense) particularly since symbolic language represses, or occludes, the semiotic disposition. It is imperative to note that language as symbolic function is precisely that, a language which maintains symbolic function. That is to say, the symbolic function is only one modality of the signifying process and the occlusion of the semiotic is, at the same time, never quite complete, that in this dialectical conflict the semiotic is differentiated and it is this gesture which allows for the restructuring of the symbolic order, and the subsequent development of a subjectivity.[42]

In the second, any account of the speaking subject and the signifying process necessarily takes into account historical conditions, since it always includes the symbolic realm of social constraints as a context.

And third, it is the notion of the materiality of language as being analogous to an expanding indifference to meaning, a polymorphous pleasure or carnality, that is, a 'sexual overdetermination', which pushes writing into that field where the discourse of the physical/psychical subject may be accounted for; that is, psychoanalysis.

ANALYSIS – WRITING – PRACTICE

What then is the relation between Kristevan semiotics and contemporary writing on art practice?

The theory of Kristevan semiotics, while focusing on the poetic text, or that manner of writing which deems itself poetic, crossing and recrossing the boundaries of genre and syntax where the activated semiotic may be apprehended, is also articulated as a practice and that practice is a semanalysis. And despite the criticism that Kristeva has incurred for her reliance on the work of the male literary persona as the subject of her own analytical writing, this does not restrict the method of semanalysis to that usage. Nor, it should be said, does this detract from the seminal value of the thesis of the acquisition of language which argues for a consideration of language not as a static object of linguistic study but as the enunciation of a (bio-physiological) speaking subject.[43]

As a method for writing about art practices the Kristevan project of semanalysis is of fundamental importance since it restores subjectivity—the profound extremity of the condition of being in the world, which is tenuous and inadmissible, the occluded space or moment which encompasses the boundaries of adversity (law) and the proximity of that which is pleasurable (materiality) in the propitiate unfolding of its many forms—to the process of analysis. This enables the analyst to engage in a textual practice which is threefold, to account for the structure of signification and the mediating role of subjectivity (necessarily gendered and different in every instance) while acknowledging his/her own intervention in that process. This has been imperative for a contemporary textual practice which sought to account for those discursive practices in which the woman is both subject and producer of culture—a practice which may then account for the sexual and emotional investment of the gendered body in that production. The procedure of semanalysis has enabled a form of writing (necessarily elliptical in its attempt to apprehend such a material process) to come into being and so account for that which was formerly unrepresentable, that is, the corporeal dimension of any particular cultural articulation, thus going beyond an archivistic art history, and in doing so place textual practice, as a speculative exegesis, at the matrix of the political.[44]

NOTES

1 J. Kristeva *Semeiotike: Recherches Pour une Semanalyse* Paris: Seuil, 1969. For an overview of the area of feminist criticism, see Toril Moi *Sexual/ Textual Politics: Feminist Literary Theory* London: Methuen, 1985. See also her *Kristeva Reader* Oxford: Blackwell, 1986, for a selection of Kristeva's writings. Two Australian accounts of her work are available: E. Grosz *Sexual Subversions: Three French Feminists* Sydney: Allen & Unwin, 1989; and John Lechte *Julia Kristeva* London: Routledge, 1990.

2 J. Kristeva *Desire in Language, A Semiotic Approach to Literature and Art* Oxford: Basil Blackwell, 1980

3 Kristeva 'The Father, Love and Banishment' in *Desire in Language* p. 148

4 ibid. p. 151

5 J. Feral 'The Powers of Difference' in H. Eisenstein and A. Jardine (eds) *The Future of Difference* Boston: Hall & Co., 1980, p. 89

6 ibid. pp. 149–50

7 ibid. p. 158

8 *Desire in Language* p. 15

9 *Desire in Language* p. viii

10 J. Kristeva *Revolution in Poetic Language* New York: Columbia University Press, 1984, pp. 167–70, 180

11 R. Jakobson *Verbal Art, Verbal Sign, Verbal Time* Oxford: Basil Blackwell, 1985

12 E. Grosz 'Julia Kristeva and the Speaking Subject' in *Sexual Subversions* p. 42. 'No social or discursive function can be understood without some notion of the speaking being as the locus of textual production and deformation.'

13 *Revolution in Poetic Language* p. 180. Described by Kristeva as 'matter in the process of splitting'.

14 *Revolution in Poetic Language* pp. 179–81

15 ibid.

16 16 *Revolution in Poetic Language*, pp. 62–67

17 R. Jakobson *Verbal Art, Verbal Sign, Verbal Time* pp. 77, 159. According to Jakobson elliptical structures are those which constantly struggle against explicit language in order to allow for a multiplicity of meaning. Jakobson distinguishes between explicit and elliptical structures by noting that 'elliptical structures are those in which certain signs are left out, while explicit structures are those fully replete with signs'.

18 R. Cohen (ed.) *Face to Face with Levinas* New York: State University of New York Press, 1986, in particular the essays in this collection entitled 'The Sensuality and the Sensitivity' by Alphonso Lingis and 'The Fecundity of the Caress' by Luce Irigaray.

19 L. Roudiez 'Introduction to Julia Kristeva' in *Desire in Language* p. 2

20 Kristeva *Desire in Language* p. 281

21 Kristeva 'The Ethics of Linguistics' in *Desire in Language* p. 31

22 ibid. p. 25

23 *Desire in Language* p. x

24 E. Grosz 'Every Picture Tells a Story: Art and Theory Re-examined' *Sighting References* Sydney: Artspace, 1987

25 *Desire in Language* p. 133. According to Kristeva the semiotic disposition is 'definitely heterogeneous to meaning but always in sight of it in either a negative or surplus relation to it'.

26 *Revolution in Poetic Language* p. 5. Leon Roudiez comments on Kristeva's attention to textual practice as oppositional to a 'literary criticism', and he notes that 'the point is to give an account of what went into the work, how it affects readers, and why. The text that is analysed is actually the effect of the dialectical interplay between the semiotic and symbolic dispositions'.

27 L. Roudiez 'Introduction to Julia Kristeva' in *Desire in Language* p. 18

28 *Desire in Language* p. x

29 ibid. p. x

30 ibid. p. vii. In her preface to Kristeva's essay entitled 'The System and the Speaking Subject', Toril Moi notes that it is by insisting on the study of language in its specific relation to the notion of a speaking subject that the basic materiality of language (language as production) is allowed for.

31 *Desire in Language*, p. x.

32 T. Moi *The Kristeva Reader* Oxford: Basil Blackwell, 1986, p. 24. Moi notes here that the 'semiotician is forced always to analyse her own discursive position'.

33 *Desire in Language* p. x. According to Kristeva the semiotician as subject takes up an active position which ensures that one is 'neither the master nor the slave of meaning'. See also the essay 'The Ethics of Linguistics'.

34 ibid. p. viii

35 ibid. p. viii

36 ibid. p. x. Kristeva gives a summary of what the condition of the subject (subjectivity) may consist of, through the notion of a 'brink'. 'The speaking being maintains himself or herself as such to the extent that s/he allows for the presence of two brinks. On the one hand there is pain—but it makes one secure—caused as one recognizes oneself as subject of (other's) discourse, hence tributary of a universal Law. On the other, there is pleasure—but it kills—at finding oneself different, irreducible, for one is borne by a simply singular speech, not merging with the others, but then exposed to the black thrusts of a desire that borders on idiolect and aphasia. In other words, if the overly constraining and reductive meaning of a language made up of universals causes us to suffer, the call of the unnameable, on the contrary, issuing from those borders where signification vanishes, hurls us into a void of psychosis that appears henceforth as the solidary reverse of our universe, saturated with interpretation, faith, and truth. Within that vice, our only chance to avoid being neither master nor slave of meaning lies in our ability to insure our mastery of (through technique or knowledge) as well as our passage through it (play or practice). In a word, jouissance.'

37 ibid. p. viii. In identifying the specific object of analysis as art practice Kristeva describes this object: 'That uncanny object, pre-text and foil, weak link in human sciences and fascinating otherness for philosophy, is none other than art in general, modern art and literature more particularly'.

38 ibid. p. viii. Kristeva refers specifically to the effect on the study of linguistics (Saussure) and philosophy (Hegel, Husserl) of this re-placement of the subject of psychoanalysis (Lacan) as an object of study.

39 *Revolution in Poetic Language* pp. 100–103. In a move which differs from Lacan's delineation of the four types of discourse (hysteric, academic, master, analyst) Kristeva posits four types of signifying practice: narrative, metalanguage, contemplation, and the text. What is of interest here is the category of the text (or art practice), for the text according to this account is the site into which instinctual drives, both continuous and discontinuous, are released in a passage through meaning by means of a practice which always exceeds that meaning. The text then is a practice which posits and breaks up semiotic matter (colour, form, line, sound, organs, words) and representation (the sign) in an endless process. Kristeva cites the paintings of Mark Rothko as an example of such a practice.

40 Kristeva 'How Does One Speak To Literature' in *Desire in Language* p. 100. While Kristeva refers here specifically to the new epistemological status of writing as it is found in the work of Roland Barthes, this statement may be used as a schematic summary of the basic principles which underlie the critical practice of semanalysis, as is noted by Leon Roudiez.

41 ibid. p. 100

42 *Desire in Language*. In the essay 'From One Identity to Another' Kristeva discusses the notion of semiotic activity (traces of the instinctual drives of appropriation/rejection, orality/anality, love/hate, life/death as they appear in writing or texts) as it occurs in a writing (poetic language) which differentiates from the symbolic function of language.

43 Moi *The Kristeva Reader* p. 24

44 *Revolution in Poetic Language* p. 13

In his chapter on Blanchot, David Odell dwells on the relation between theory and fiction. He contrasts the style of *nouvelle roman* with immanent presentation of theory contained in Blanchot's *récits*. In controversial mode, Odell places Blanchot's writing in the context of Hegel, and speaks of the presence of a 'gnostic sublime' for which only some readers might find 'resonance'. Should philosophy have such a personal reading?

DAVID ODELL

3 An introduction to Maurice Blanchot

The word 'theory' has become customary to describe a certain more systematic, self-conscious, and philosophically informed discourse which seems to have emerged by lateral displacement from literary criticism. A geographically sensitive history of the dissemination of this usage would doubtless reveal a dual anxiety, to contain and to preserve certain impulses; as well as the more telling effects of a necessary misprision which mean that the word is never understood the same way twice, even when it has apparently ceased to be a matter of contention. Let us begin, however, by hearing Maurice Blanchot,[1] who has been described as one of the godfathers of that motley phenomenon which we so readily identify as French theoretical discourse, addressing the theorists in a recent text:

> Enough of theory which wields and organizes knowledge. Here space opens to 'fictive theory', and theory, through fiction, comes into danger of dying. You theoreticians know that you are mortal, and that theory is already death in you. Know this, be acquainted with your companion. Perhaps it is true that 'without theorizing, you would not take one step forward,' but this step is one more step toward the abyss of truth. Thence rises the silent murmuring, the tacit intensity.[2]

The hyperbolic diction is immediately recognisable to readers of the genre, but one might stop to wonder about the invocation of 'silent murmuring, [and] tacit intensity' in the face of what must often seem a project whose particular frissons arise within the very excesses of language. Indeed Blanchot's tone here (and elsewhere) is more prophetic than that to which we are generally accustomed, and yet in this it has gone largely unchallenged by the younger generation of French thinkers, those who came to the fore in the sixties, to some extent as the conscious heirs of the circle of thinkers which included Blanchot as well as Georges Bataille, Michel Leiris, and Pierre Klossowski. In Blanchot we must be prepared to encounter the difficulty of a figure authorised to speak for silence, one who, with all the quasi-theological connotations that this entails, has his dwelling and his obsession with precisely that unrepresentable core 'where words break off' which the various deconstructions ceaselessly evoke.

Not very much is known about Maurice Blanchot. The French dictionary of literary biography tells us only that he was born in the provinces in September 1907. There are no known photographs, and he has never lectured or given readings or interviews. At the beginning of his most recently published text, the posthumous appreciation of Michel Foucault, entitled 'Michel Foucault As I Imagine Him', which appeared together with a 1966 text of Foucault's entitled 'Maurice Blanchot: The Thought From Outside' in a book called *Foucault/Blanchot* in 1986, he appends 'A few personal words' in which he plays with his own anonymity:

> Let me say first of all that I had no personal relations with Michel Foucault. I never met him, except one time, in the courtyard of the Sorbonne, during the events of May '68, perhaps in June or July (but I was later told he wasn't there), when I addressed a few words to him, he himself unaware of who was speaking to him . . . [3]

Blanchot's career as a writer had begun 30 years before this with the right-wing polemics which he contributed to the short-lived journal *Combat* (not to be confused with the later use of this name by the Communist Party). The American critics, Jeffrey Mehlman[4] and Allan Stoekl,[5] in studies of this earliest incarnation of Blanchot and of its supersession, have put forward the argument that the 'silence' which Blanchot continually evokes from the moment in the early forties when he emerges as a literary theorist and precursor of deconstruction is far more specific and interested than it seems. It can be seen as the guilty silence behind which an unacceptable past is masked and secretly preserved in a way which tacitly places the complicity of the entire deconstructive movement into question. This view of Blanchot, which I have perhaps made seem more reductive than it is, cannot be ignored, especially as it connects up with the larger re-evaluation of deconstruction which has been prompted by the rediscovery of Paul de Man's collaborationist writings and the renewal of interest in Heidegger's Nazi sympathies. In Blanchot's case, however, at least as much as in any other, I think it wise to read the 'either/or' of his accusers by way of his own more complex motives for evasion, such as are hinted at in this passage from the seminal *récit* of 1948, *La Folie du Jour*:

> I had been asked: Tell us *'just* exactly' what happened. A story? I began: I am not learned; I am not ignorant. I have known joys. That is saying too little. I told them the whole story and they listened, it seems to me, with interest, at least in the beginning. But the end was a surprise to all of us. 'That was the beginning,' they said. 'Now get down to the facts.' How so? The story was over![6]

(It is perhaps also worth mentioning that during the occupation Blanchot refused the directorship of the prestigious *Nouvelle Revue Française* when it was offered to him by a former colleague who was by then employed by Vichy, and who attempted to persuade him that he would be given a perfectly free hand.)[7]

From the forties until almost the present Blanchot has pursued a triple career: as a prominent literary journalist writing weekly or monthly essays on the writers or thinkers of European modernism; as a writer of fiction, at first of novels relatively conventional in form but later of a type of fictional text which he has particularly championed against the novel, the *récit*; and finally as what we are forced by the limitations of our language to call a theoretician, one who relentlessly pursues a meditation, by turns discursive and expository, polemical, or aphoristic and personal, at times with an eye to the monuments and recurrent obsessions of philosophy and at others seeming to strain at the fabric of history.

Despite his prominence in France through the fifties and sixties it is only since the late seventies that the bulk of his work has begun to be translated into English. He has been 'discovered' as a precursor to the post-structuralists, and indeed it is only in this way that we have been able to perceive the peculiar register of ideas in which he works. It is hard to imagine a reception anything like that which Sartre received, for example, although in certain respects Blanchot stood at the opposite pole from Sartre, defining the position from which the later anti-humanisms would fire their salvos. Thus Blanchot's seminal essay 'Literature and the Right to Death' was in some sense a reply to Sartre's 'What is Literature?'.

The translations of Blanchot which are now starting to appear mostly come from America, where there seems to be mounting interest in his work among the literary/academic avant-garde. The first printings of each new volume of Blanchot to come off the presses nowadays seem to be sold out almost immediately. Most of the fiction has been produced by small presses such as Station Hill Press in New York State, and the 'theoretical' texts by university presses such as Nebraska and Columbia. His books are becoming easier to find in local specialty bookshops. Lydia Davis, who has translated Blanchot for Station Hill Press and Columbia University Press, is herself the author of a number of fascinating minimal fictions published by various small presses in the USA.

I would like to give you some idea of what Blanchot's fictions or *récits* are like, but I must say that I find myself initially at a loss to do so since their very essence is bound up with the way that they repel similitude or paraphrase. Derrida, who has devoted a long-running seminar to certain of the *récits* of Blanchot, says somewhere[8] that entering one of these texts is like finding oneself lost in a dim and misty landscape which is occasionally illumined by vast beams of light from an unlocatable lighthouse. They certainly do not bear the same relation to his critical writings that, say, the *nouveau roman* writers bore to Barthes' critical championing of them. Blanchot is his own theorist, but the relation between his texts and meta-texts is by no means evident. Indeed these two bodies of writing stand back to back, never mentioning each other, and yet nonetheless seem mutually to incite the reader, the one with its incessant meditations on the moment of writing, the very act of writing as a version of death, and the other with its peculiar Kafkaesque spatialisations in which every line, as a version of that separating life and death, is erased with terrifying ease by a language just that much more aware of itself than the imaginary limits of narrative seem able to accommodate.

A comparison with the *nouveau roman* is perhaps instructive. Although they may initially appear to share a certain strangeness, greater familiarity reveals a wholly different narrative desire. Blanchot's *récits* are indelibly strange, like a Klein bottle. They are difficult in a way that seems unassimilable to any higher motives of realism, for example, in contrast to the way that the *nouveau roman* has by now become part of the general expressive idiom of novelistic prose, and even of cinema (to which it was always closely tied by a certain dialectic of voyeurism). Another way of getting at this might be to say that Blanchot works within and against the Hegelian phenomenology whereas the *nouveau roman* emerges from problematics of Husserlian phenomenology.

Blanchot's relation to Hegel is absolutely crucial. It would only be a slight exaggeration to say that ever since Mallarmé the strangest texts of French literature have been in part creative (mis)readings of Hegel. Indeed, despite the fact that the French were comparatively late[9] in taking up the study of Hegelian philosophy with the Kojève circle of the 1930s, one might venture the idea that Hegel, as the (true?) philosopher of the Napoleonic period, resumes the momentum if not the ideas of the French eighteenth-century thinkers. In 'Literature and the Right to Death', Blanchot gives a reading of the negation inherent in imagination and writing according to his own unrecuperated version of the dialectic. At a crucial point of the essay he connects the development of this negation with the Reign of Terror which followed the events of 1789, quoting Hegel on the death which was then so widely dealt: 'It is thus the coldest and meanest of all deaths, with no more significance than cutting off a head of cabbage or swallowing a mouthful of water'. Blanchot goes on to become the most subtle philosopher of that death, really the one death, which cannot any longer be disguised by such terms as 'the good death'. This is especially so in his major recent works, *Le pas au-delà* ('The Step [or The No] Beyond'), (1973) and *L'Ecriture du désastre* ('The Writing of the Disaster' 1980). But I want to go back for a moment to the idea of fictions which draw on the Phenomenology of the Subject rather than on that of Consciousness because I think that, albeit superficially, this helps us to grasp some of the strangeness and fascination of Blanchot's *récits*.

Imagine a fictional, written world haunted by a notion of Absolute Knowledge, but unable to say whether it is infinitely distant or infinitely close. One thinks perhaps of Kafka, and rightly so. Imagine a subjectivity in such a text which is not a correlative of its horizon, but rather—since it is subject to the infinitely deferred indeed impossible irruption of a Knowledge which would overturn all of its defining, moulding its shadows into light—is indeterminately identical with that horizon, with what would normally be the matrix of the non-self. Imagine a narrative voice of a paradoxical lucidity which can make the starkest reversals of sense seem a necessity.

A short passage from near the beginning of *The Last Man* (1957) might illustrate the strange ontology this entails. The 'I' character is describing the eponymous 'last man':

> At these times, he talks very fast in a sort of low voice: great
> sentences that seem infinite, that roll with the sound of waves, an
> all-encompassing murmur, a barely perceptible planetary song. This
> goes on and on, is terribly imposing in its gentleness and distance.
> How to answer? Listening to it, who wouldn't have the feeling of
> being that target?
>
> He wasn't addressing anyone. I don't mean he wasn't speaking
> to me, but someone other than me was listening to him, someone

who was perhaps richer, vaster, and yet more singular, almost too general, as though, confronting him, what had been 'I' had strangely awakened into a 'we', the presence and united force of the common spirit. I was a little more, a little less than myself: more, in any case, than all men. In this 'we', there is the earth, the power of the elements, a sky that is not this sky, there is a feeling of loftiness and calm, there is also the bitterness of an obscure constraint. All of this is I before him, and he seems almost nothing at all.

Blanchot finds one of his paradigms of the *récit* in *Moby Dick*, which he contrasts with *The Odyssey* as the paradigm of the novel: 'We cannot deny that Ulysses understood something of what Ahab saw, but he stood fast within that understanding, while Ahab became lost in the image'. The novel elaborates the details and perspectives of 'the voyage which takes Ulysses to the moment of the encounter'; it relishes details and sidetracks. What the *récit* approaches is the *récit* itself: it is an allegory of itself. It takes upon itself the full measure of its own always already deconstructedness. 'The *récit* is not the narration of an event, but that event itself, the approach to that event, the place where that event is made to happen—an event which is yet to come and through whose power of attraction the *récit* can hope to come into being too.'

This distinction between novel and *récit* raises questions about Blanchot's meta-texts as (potential) criticism. Is this a distinction which can be maintained outside the hothouse world of Blanchot's late-late-modernism? Or indeed might it have some value for French literary culture, as one approach to a division which can at any rate be made out in a number of historical sections, but would lead us only to irrelevant criteria in, for example, the local context? One answer to the accusation of baroque obscurantism which can be levelled at much of Blanchot's deeper writings on writing is that while they may be expressed in a general way they are in fact responses only to certain privileged texts, a company from which, for example, Sartre's novels seem to be excluded. Does this merely reflect his taste? The following sentence, which is from 'Literature and the Right to Death', gives us some clue to Blanchot's criterion. It comes after granting that 'literature is built on its own ruins', that is, that literary creation is inseparable from a breaking down of its own structures:

> But we must still ask whether the challenge brought against art by the most illustrious works of art of the last thirty years is not based on a redirection, the displacement, of a force labouring in the secrecy of works and loath to emerge into broad daylight, a

force the thrust of which was originally quite distinct from any depreciation of literary activity or the literary Thing.[10]

I shall not attempt a commentary on this—in a sense Blanchot's critical *oeuvre* is just that, but it seems to me quite possible that in hearing these words you might feel a certain dark resonance, and be drawn to the recognition or the memory, in certain literary texts, of an absent presence from which a sort of wild dispersal seems to radiate, something which goes way beyond such clichés as 'imaginative power', 'self-referentiality', 'alienation-effect', or even 'pursuit of excellence'. If this seems meaningless then I suspect that Blanchot has nothing for you, but if it doesn't then you may agree with me that some of the recent writing which has appeared in this country has been pushing (necessarily by taking on a kind of blindness) into this very region. This does not mean that we are actually able to read Blanchot here, or that we shall at some future moment discover that he is inescapable. The textual ecology, if I can use such a term, which sustains his particular discourse remains at a far greater remove from us than a spate of translations and more or less eager introductions might lead us to believe. We do, however, inherit some claim to the landscape.

One of the dimensions of this remoteness, and this is more or less the final thing I want to talk about, as it comes closest to Blanchot as 'theorist', is the relation to Hegel. A simple slogan which for me captures much of this relation, although it applies equally well, or better, to Georges Bataille, is that Blanchot is a sort of Hegelian gnostic. He is the practitioner of a dialectic which substitutes *katabasis* or descent for *Aufhebung*. If we could essentialise the idea of gnostic revision it would run something like this: an impassioned and necessarily fragmentary counter-discourse which emerges out of the gaps which historical crisis has exposed in some prior synthesis— whether of philosophy or religion—which has attained cosmological dimensions and ontological positivity, and which, while remaining obsessively attached to the terms of that prior synthesis, strategically reverses certain of them to initiate its own non-totalisable trajectory of antithetical insight. One could say it was deconstruction without scepticism.[11]

The Writing of the Disaster does this most explicitly. 'The Disaster', which is the term he uses as a touchstone for thinking, a stone which rolls through the book's various paragraphs without gathering moss, is etymologised to yield a realm displaced from the 'sidereal', which is precisely the universe where exchange and meaning have their values, where the 'labour of the negative' is historically recuperated. For both Bataille and Blanchot the Hegelian 'labour of the negative' is a crux. As Frenchmen of the twentieth century, their sense of the negative is likely to have been keener than even Hegel could imagine. In particular, for Blanchot, the negatives on which he meditates are those named 'consciousness' and 'writing'. To the Hegelian negative Blanchot opposes the 'neutral'. He invokes the prospect of two languages, one dialectical and the other not so, the one working, the other belonging to 'worklessness' (a literal rendering of *désoeuvrement*, a term Blanchot uses for the inner nature of the work of art). For the dialectic, negativity is the task. The neutral remains apart, cut off from both being and non-being. These represent two claims upon us. Blanchot's is a rigorous attempt to write the logic of the neutral, the un-working negative. To attempt this is to set language to work and thus to appear necessarily to have failed. But language is so intimately connected to the effacing passivity of the neutral that the writing of the neutral has already begun long before this failure has been suspected and is its presupposition: 'To fail without fail: this is a sign of passivity'.[12] 'Passivity' names the movement which undoes dialectical recuperation; it is the falling or dispersal which paradoxically completes the work, theorised elsewhere as the Gaze of Orpheus, or again as the truth in death which refutes, for example, that concept of death which the will claims in suicide.

> Never either-or, simple logic. And never two at once, the two that always end up affirming each other dialectically or compulsively (antagonism without any risk to it). All dualism, all binaries draw thought into the conveniences of exchanges: the accounts will all be settled. Eros Thanatos: two forces yet again . . . There is not the death drive; the throes of death are thefts from unity, lost multitudes.[13]

The Writing of the Disaster is also an attempt to write from a sense of the disastrous in history. This is a time when disaster crowds history, so that discourse seems to be marked either by an excess of forgetfulness or by a too loud remembering, both perhaps 'sidereal' strategies for recuperating meaning. It is not so much that Blanchot seeks to create a writing that can dwell in or lose itself in disaster, as that writing for him is already this. *The Writing of the Disaster* brings a certain ethical dimension of this to the fore whose power to move us should not make us forget its sources in a kind of gnostic sublime. I shall let Blanchot have the last word, from 'Literature and the Right to Death':

A novelist writes in the most transparent kind of prose, he describes men we could have met ourselves and actions we could have performed; he says his aim is to express the reality of a human world the way Flaubert did. In the end, though, his work really has only one subject. What is it? The horror of existence deprived of the world, the process through which whatever ceases to be continues to be, whatever is forgotten is always answerable to memory, whatever dies encounters only the impossibility of dying, whatever seeks to attain the beyond is always still here. This process is day which has become fatality, consciousness whose light is no longer the lucidity of the vigil but the stupor of lack of sleep, it is existence without being, as poetry tries to recapture it behind the meaning of words, which reject it.[14]

NOTES

1 Blanchot's theoretical writings in English are the following: *The Gaze of Orpheus, and other literary essays* transl. Lydia Davis, New York: Station Hill Press, 1981 (This volume includes the essay 'Literature and the Right to Death'); *The Writing of the Disaster* transl. Ann Smock, University of Nebraska, 1986; *Foucault/Blanchot* transl. Mehlman and Massumi, New York: Zone Press, 1987; *The Space of Literature* transl. Ann Smock, University of Nebraska, 1982; *The Uncommunity* transl. Lydia Davis, New York: Station Hill, 1988; *The Beast of Lascaux* transl. David Odell, (forthcoming); *The Siren's Song* transl. Gabriel Josipovici Brighton: Harvester Press, 1982. His fictional writings in English are: *The Madness of the Day* transl. Lydia Davis, New York: Station Hill, 1981; *Death Sentence* transl. Lydia Davis, New York: Station Hill, 1978; *Vicious Circles, two fictions & 'after the fact'* transl. Paul Auster, New York: Station Hill, 1985; *When the Time Comes* transl. Lydia Davis, New York: Station Hill, 1985; *The Last Man* transl. Lydia Davis, New York: Columbia University Press, 1988; *Thomas the Obscure* transl. Robert Lamberton, (reprint forthcoming from Station Hill Press). A place to begin a reading of Blanchot's theory is *The Gaze of Orpheus,* and good starting places for his fiction are *Death Sentence* and *Thomas the Obscure.*

2 *Writing of the Disaster* p. 43

3 *Foucault/Blanchot* p. 63

4 *Legacies of Anti-Semitism in France* Minneapolis: University of Minnesota Press, 1983

5 *Politics, Writing, Mutilation: The cases of Bataille, Blanchot, Roussel, Leiris, and Ponge* Minneapolis: University of Minnesota Press, 1985

6 *The Madness of the Day* p. 18

7 Blanchot details this in a letter addressed to Jeffrey Mehlman in November 1979 and quoted in part in a postscript to his book, p. 117.

8 *Parages* Paris: Gallilée, 1986

9 British Hegelianism, for example, had pretty much died out by the turn of the century, and seems to have had negligible literary impact, unless one cares to argue for a line through Bradley to Eliot.

10 *Gaze of Orpheus* p. 22
11 Or in fairness to the latter, a precursor of deconstruction in flight from the trials of scepticism.
12 *Writing and Disaster* p. 11
13 ibid. p. 46
14 *Gaze of Orpheus* p. 52

PART II
Reading

More than most, Roland Barthes extended his focus outside the academic archive and drew into consideration what seem unofficial *personal* experiences, such as leaving a movie theatre and walking streets at night. At the same time, the subjective understanding of the personal was denied by a broadening of the semiotic dimension to an understanding of *authorship*, per se. Viriginia Trioli's experiment with the personal and theoretical in her chapter on Barthes can be read as an expression of one of the places where both these moments might lead.

4 Roland Barthes
Autobiography in spite of myself

By virtue of their currency,
the other authors discussed in
these papers do not need their presence justified.
But like the vigilant father who does not know
when to take his leave,
Roland Barthes is almost an unwelcome guest here.
Roland Barthes set down in the sixties and seventies
the principles of structuralism and post-structuralism
that became the basic grammar of
narrative theory and the critical discourses of
semiotics and deconstruction.

His words and his images became incorporated into the
bedrock of critical language and cultural theory, with
books such as *Empire of the Signs*, *Writing Degree Zero*
and *The Pleasure of the Text*. These works have not only
assumed the monumental status they have today as modern
classics of critical thought, but they have become a
terminology in themselves, another language that we
must demand access to. Another set of buzz words to learn.

I

Roland Barthes[1] was his own best subject matter. He championed
the arrival of the reader over the departure of the author, by killing
off the author as an authoritative voice, yet he eventually came to
write in a language that knows and recognises a 'person' and not

only a 'subject'.[2] He shifted from averting his eyes from the mark left by the author on the page *(Death of the Author* 1968), to listening out for the "Grain of the Voice": 'the only erotic part of a pianist's body, the pad of the fingers whose grain is so rarely heard'.[3] Upon hearing Barthes' voice in a text, I am not directed to construct it as a disembodied character within that text—as he would elsewhere have the reader do. I am instead invited to a reunion between himself and his memory, where Barthes acts as Master of Ceremonies.

I I

Who can blame us when we find we have fallen into the gap that is left between the voice and the image?

I I I

Until about 1973, Barthes insisted on a distance that should necessarily exist between the writer and reader. He exacts upon his own pleasure in reading, a denial of history—the history that would underpin the 'collective biography' that his later works would comprise.

I do not know where there has ever been a hedonist aesthetics. Certainly there exists a pleasure of the work—of certain works. I can delight in reading then re-reading Proust, Flaubert, Balzac and even—why not?—Alexander Dumas. But this pleasure, no matter how keen, and even when free from all prejudice, remains in part (unless by some exceptional critical effort) a pleasure of consumption, for if I can read these authors, I also know that I cannot re-write them (that it is impossible today to write like that), and this knowledge, depressing enough, suffices to cut me off from the production of these works, in the very moment their remoteness establishes my modernity.[4]

I V

Christian Metz says: In the darkness of a cinema a dirty old man slips his hand onto the thigh of the woman sitting next to him. She exclaims, 'You disgusting old man! Be so good as to remove your hand! I'll give you ten minutes, not a second more'.

V

Roland Barthes says, 'Don't, stop; don't stop' in a denial of intimacy that characterises the split he identifies in his writing: the voice that creates and that which criticises. The writer who observes against the lingual lover who is involved.[5]

It is language itself, its palpability and its ability to *contain* that Barthes struggles with as he inscribes himself over and over onto the page. This incongruity is accompanied by a fear at the effect of his double discourse; that although the aim of his discourse is not truth, it is assertive. Barthes feared his private language would become reduced to the method through which he would make the authority of his voice tremble.[6]

'Henceforth, I would have to consent to combine two voices: the voice of banality (to say what everyone sees and knows) and the voice of singularity (to replenish such banality with all the elan of an emotion which belonged only to myself).'[7]

V I

How can I identify the moment of indifference that separates the fascination of the writer for the reader, from that which fascinates the writer?

V I I

Italo Calvino speaks of the irritated subjectivity of the author, the gaze that repeatedly turns inwards in spite of oneself. When this becomes too singular, when the multiplicity of voices that comprise the densely layered text is sliced down to the one persistent voice, there is little room left for the reader. Then the author is left to occupy that textual space alone.[8]

V I I I

I, I, the filthiest of all the pronouns! The pronouns! They are the lice of thought. When a thought has lice it scratches, and in your fingernails then, you find pronouns: the personal pronouns.[9]

I X

The writer tries to attract the reader. This is not autobiography. This is (multiple) exposure of the image. The writer does not resort to a language too private or removed. The writer adopts a tone of voice that is singular, particular. Through this, the writer's self bleeds into the text. Discreetly. The writer knows that when the specific representation of self occurs, and in so doing excludes the reader (the silent reader kept still between the pages), then once and for all the open text slams shut, and its illimitable proliferation of images is blocked. The reader is denied the pleasure of inscribing her history onto the history that the writer unravels; her ludic truth,[10] which through her bodily gesture of reading, posits and perverts the order of the text in one and the same movement.[11]

X

This is not a book of 'confessions'; not that it is insincere, but because we have a different knowledge today than yesterday; such knowledge can be summarised as follows: what I write about myself is never the *last word*: the more 'sincere' I am, the more interpretable I am, under the eye of other examples than those of the old authors, who believed they were required to submit themselves to but one law; *authenticity*.[12]

XI

I read *A Lover's Discourse* during my first year at university. I stumbled around the campus clutching my dog-eared copy, breathlessly leaping through the process from desire to torment, to waiting, waiting. A friend happened upon me and asked what I was reading. I showed him. He sniffed;—Isn't that the book where Barthes finds 24 different ways of saying the same thing over and over?

This made me very nervous.

I had not noticed the repetition. I did not know if that was bad. I was not bored. I wonder if perhaps it was not enough to read this book murmuring all the while 'yes, yes, it was like that for me too'.

XII

Is it possible to write oneself into being?
How can you crystallise memory
into the hard quartz of narrative?

XIII

'The 'I' which writes the text, it too is never more
than a paper 'I'.,[13]

XIV

I leave a telephone message for a friend at their place of work. I spell my name for the person who takes the message, and he uses it to say goodbye. There is an awkward moment just before we hang up, as if an invitation to converse has been extended with the use of my name. We both hesitate before replacing the receiver.

XV

But Roland Barthes was willing to position himself as a speaking subject within the text, not merely as an authorial voice within the text that Barthes himself speaks. He becomes a Proper Name, allowing the voice/the body/the texts to conflate to create the name. It is with the discussion of language, in particular the languages created by writers he admires most—Sade, Proust, Requichot, Brillat-Savarin—and the palpable eroticism of his own language, that Barthes inscribes his presence. For finally the body of Roland moves into the space of the readerly: the muscles, bones and viscera of an extraordinarily fleshy writer. The 'imaging' of his own body, however, is not always the point of these discussions, but instead another system of representation is employed. And in imagining himself, Barthes speaks of the writers, the painters he admires in the language of the gastronome. He allows luscious descriptions of painting, fiction and paradox to spill over with his metaphors of cooking, eating, digesting.

Barthes speaks of systems of change as does a chef on the making of a sauce.

Have you ever watched the preparation of a Swiss dish called Raclette? A hemisphere of raw cheese is held vertically over the grille; it melts, swells and sizzles; the knife gently scrapes this liquid blister, this runny surplus from the shape; it fall like a white dung; it hardens, it yellows on the plate; with the knife the amputated area is smoothed out; and then the process begins all over again. This is, strictly speaking an operation of painting. For in painting, as in cooking, *something must be allowed to drop somewhere* . . . [14]

XVI

'*In what he writes, there are two texts. Text I is reactive, moved by indignations, fears, unspoken rejoinders, minor paranoias, defenses, scenes. Text II is active, moved by pleasure. But as it is written, corrected, accommodated to the fiction of Style, Text I becomes active too, whereupon it loses its reactive skin, which subsists only in patches (mere parentheses).'[15]*

As Barthes exacts his own pleasure on the text in this way, he becomes something of the loving artisan who wounds and ruptures the surface of the material, in order to wrest it from images of its process.

This process of movement between the two texts that Barthes described is not one of reconciliation within the realm of the 'readerly'. Barthes does not apply the principles of non-contradiction and multiplying solidarities[16] in order to 'hold' everything together within a readable discourse. He describes this obsession with the logical discourse as defensive and suspicious, preparing as it does its own defense against possible 'disturbances of the text'.[17]

Instead, Barthes indicates in this small germ of self-description a project that relies upon a friction between two discourses, a scuffing that occurs within the text's own contradictions. It is a process whereby the two discourses emerge as parallel texts, initially both prickling against each other and eventually emerging as the two speaking voices Barthes no longer feels the need to justify.

XVII

The strand of fiction that binds discourse is terribly strong. It holds together the fragile monologues of autobiography we demand from the writer. The reader plucks at its threads—threads of stories she once spoke herself.

XVIII

While Barthes is prepared to admit the collision of his two languages, the critical and the creative, he makes no promises that the two will be kept separate. Often the protuberances of his body keep falling into the text.

XIX

In the skillet, the oil spreads, flat, matte: a kind of *materia prima*. Drop a slice of potato into it; it is like a morsel tossed to the wild beasts only half asleep, waiting. They all fling themselves upon it, attack it noisily: a voracious banquet. The slice of potato is surrounded—not destroyed, but hardened, caramelised, made crisp;

it becomes an object: a French-fried potato. This is how, on any object, a good language system *functions*, attacks, surrounds, sizzles, hardens and browns. All languages are microsystems of ebullition, of frying. That is the state of linguistic *mache*. The language of others transforms me into a pomme fritte.[18]

X X

How not to speak about what you really love, while not speaking about yourself.

'This morning I received a badge in the mail, *"I'm an intellectual, how about you?"* My first thought is to wear another one, very prominently: *"Don't worry about me"* '.[19]

X X I

Is Barthes trying to resurrect the author who died at his hand, and accept his own presence within the text?

It is the resonances of memory and desire that Barthes identifies in that grain, the trace elements of past stories, lingering moments of eroticism that the passage from work to text normally removes. But if the *exact* text that Barthes also desires (one that he identifies as coming from the workshop of the journal, from memory to page) is still to retain the imprint of another, then his recourse to the multiple voice, the schizophrenia of autobiography is the solution. He can privilege his almost idolatrous love of language and words over the pure trajectory of idea > narrator > reader >.

X X I I

We do not have to name our obsession, but our fictions allow us access to the unutterably intimate language in which it speaks.

I had known for quite some time, for years, that Stendhal's novel *The Charterhouse of Parma* held great treasure for me. It was a conclusion I had drawn over time, after so many sightings, mentions, references, glimpses of its title.

For I had never seen it. I had never opened a copy and knew nothing of its story. But I had kept this novel stored away in my mind, just as we confidently store books on our shelves, unopened, unread, knowing that we will get to them one day. And I knew, with each oblique encounter of its title, that I would one day be led to the book itself, and it would hold for me riches, answers: it would be a keeper of secrets.

One Saturday afternoon I was reading a collection of unremembered essays and, yet again, I fell across a reference to Stendhal's novel.

I said, 'You know, there is a strange pattern of coincidence in my life with a book I have never read. Every now and again I run into it in another story, another text, and I'm waiting for the moment to arrive when I can actually open and read the book. And when I do, it's going to make sense of everything else I've been reading for the last ten years. I know it.'

She said, 'Which book?'

'*The Charterhouse of Parma.*'

She said, 'You're kidding.'

'No, really, it's fate.'

She said, 'No, I mean all this. It's a joke on me, right?'

'What are you talking about?'

'Because you've looked over at what I'm reading, yes?'

I said, 'What the hell are you reading? I have no idea.'

She blinked and started to read from the page she had moments earlier turned to. It was from Italo Calvino's *The Literature Machine.*

> How many new readers will approach Stendhal's novel thinking of the new filmed version of 'The Charterhouse of Parma' that is shortly to appear on television? Perhaps very few in comparison with the number of viewers, or maybe a great number when matched against the statistics for readers of books in Italy. But no statistics will be able to provide us with the most important datum: how many young people will be overwhelmed from the very first pages, and be suddenly convinced that the most wonderful novel in the world could be only this one, and recognise it as the novel they have always wanted to read and one that will be a touchstone for all the novels they read in the future.

'You have to get that book.'

'Now?'

'Yes.'

I got up and went to the phone. I knew a second-hand shop that would have a copy, that it would have been sitting on the shelf, that it was still sitting on the shelf, waiting for me.

I replaced the phone. We got into the car. They were holding the copy for me. The only copy.

She said to me as I got out of the double-parked car, 'and you know that now you're going to be obsessed for the next ten years with whoever's name you find written inside that book . . . '

I carried the copy home in my hands, holding it as you would a basketball that had fallen into your lap while sitting on the sidelines of a game.

'What do I do now?'

'You read it.'

But I went and made coffee, trying to figure out what I was getting myself into.

She came out into the kitchen, a little grim.

'*One Always Fails in Speaking about What One Loves.*'

'What?'

She said, 'I've just finished reading that Calvino essay. You want to know what it's about?'

And she read me:

'*One Always Fails in Speaking about What One Loves*'. *This phrase provided the theme and the title for the last essay of Roland Barthes, which he was to have read at the Stendhal conference in Milan in March 1980; but while he was writing it he was involved in the car accident that cost him his life.*

And she said to me: 'So you will tell this story at your talk, yes?'

XXIII

'*Dear Friend,*

'*Thanks for "La Chambre Claire", which is at once a very beautiful and a luminous book. It astonishes me that you say in Chapter Three that you are a 'subject bandied back and forth between two languages, one expressive, the other critical', and that you confirm the opinion at your extraordinary first lecture at the Collège de France.*

'*But what is the artist also if not a subject bandied back and forth between two languages, one which expresses and one which does not?*

'*It was always like that. The inexorable and the inexplicable drama of artistic creation . . .*'

I was in the process of writing this letter when the news of the death of R.B. came by telephone. I did not know that he had had an accident and I felt the breath knocked out of me, and an acute sadness. The first thing that came to mind was this: 'So, there's a little less sweetness and intelligence in the world now. A bit less love. All the love which, *through living and writing*, he put into his life and his work.'

I believe that the longer we process in this world (a world which regresses brutally), the more we shall miss the virtues which were his.[20]

Michaelangelo Antonioni

XXIV

Like the writer whose memory must undergo the passage from journal to text, this is the distillation of the permitted memory—of the subject who is ordered to speak, in self-description. Another pronoun.

An autobiography in spite of myself.

NOTES

1 A concise outline of Barthes' theoretical positions is contained in a chapter by John Sturrock 'Roland Barthes' in J. Sturrock (ed.) *Structuralism and Since: From Lévi-Strauss to Derrida* Oxford: Oxford University Press, 1979. English readers usually begin reading Barthes in his *Mythologies* London: Jonathan Cape, 1972.

2 R. Barthes 'The Death of the Author' in S. Heath (ed.) *Image, Music, Text* London: Fontana, 1978, p. 145

3 ibid. p. 189

4 R. Barthes 'From Work to Text' in *The Rustle of Language* New York: Hill & Wang, 1986, p. 67

5 For further discussion of this see Andrew Preston's excellent article, 'Self/Criticism' *Intervention/Flesh* 21/22, 1988

6 Heath *Image, Music, Text* p. 48

7 R. Barthes *Camera Lucida* London: Fontana, 1984, p. 76

8 Italo Calvino *Six Notes for the Next Millennium* Harvard University Press, 1988, p. 105

9 Calvino *Six Notes* p. 106

10 R. Barthes 'Writing Reading' in *Rustle* p. 31

11 R. Barthes 'On Reading' in *Rustle* p. 36

12 *Roland Barthes by Roland Barthes* London: Macmillan, 1977, p. 120

13 R. Barthes 'From Work to Text' in *Rustle* p. 62

14 R. Barthes 'Requichot and His Body' in *The Responsibility of Forms* London: Farrar, Strauss & Giroux, 1955, p. 214

15 *Barthes by Barthes* p. 43

16 See further R. Barthes *S/Z: An Essay* New York: Hill & Wang, 1974, p. 156.

17 ibid. p. 156

18 R. Barthes 'The Image' in *Rustle* p. 355

19 R. Barthes 'Day by Day with Roland Barthes' in Marshal Blonsky (ed.) *On Signs* London: Basil Blackwell, 1985, p. 100

20 Michaelangelo Antonioni, reprinted in *L'Aventura* New Jersey: Rutgers University Press, 1989, pp. 209–14

Henry Krips points to a very particular involvement of the reader in Foucault's *History of Sexuality*, vol. 1. Foucault's story is about the construction of the reader's self: how we have become liberated from the sexual repressions of the Victorian era, etc. Is this a story we can be liberated from? What kind of story do we become part of then? Krips considers the limits of Foucault's analysis.

5 The Self unmade ... a meditation on Volume 1 of Michel Foucault's *History of Sexuality*

Hoc enim proprie vivit quod est sine principio.
Only that which is without a principal properly lives.
Meister Eckhart[1]

Volume 1 of Foucault's *History of Sexuality*[2] has a doubly disruptive impact. It provides not only an intellectual challenge to ideas of self and history but also employs its lush rhetoric to transform readers as it mobilises their engagement with the text. The text shimmers in a haze of contradictory fragments and subtle ironies which seek not so much to 'inform' as to tease, provoke, interrogate and disrupt. As readers are persuaded to enter they must join themselves to a new play, and surrender innocent Enlightenment dreams of complete description and rigorous explanation. The text implies and constructs readers who, while speaking into its silences and entering its absences, recognise that such tasks are always and already incomplete. Readers must reconstruct themselves as those who are charged with the (impossible) tasks of both completing the text and themselves. Foucauldian subjects must make themselves by realising their own unmaking.

> For a long time, the story goes, we supported a Victorian regime, and we continue to be dominated by it even today.[3]

Consider Foucault's provocative phrase 'the story goes'. Does this signal that the work at hand is to be a 'story', his-story (Foucault's story)? Or is it to be history in the more traditional sense of facts about the past, or perhaps facts about stories *we* tell about the past? It is closest to the last of these. Foucault is interested in history as

63

our discourse about the past; history as part of the medium in which we are constituted, which speaks us as we speak it, history as the stories we tell about the past, through which we tell ourselves. But he is also interested in history in the more traditional sense, as facts about the past. His own 'stories' are always a disruptive mixture of these various 'histories': our own myths slightly displaced, refracted back to us through the medium of Foucault's truth. They not only tell us what we say about our past, but also initiate a critique of those stories by enabling us to 'see through' them in some way.[4]

A sweeping chronology is introduced in the second paragraph of p. 1: 'At the beginning of the seventeenth century a certain frankness was still common, it would seem'. This is absurd history: what period is Foucault referring to, what country, what socioeconomic grouping? Foucault's text rescues itself from this absurdity by implying, indeed constructing, a special readership for itself, 'we' who not only understand and recognise the story Foucault is telling as *our* story but also recognise it *as a story*. Foucault's text examines this 'folk history' in terms of which we, who are selected and select ourselves to be his readers, construct our past and hence ourselves.

The pre-seventeenth century is figured in the story as a time of a 'tolerant familiarity with the illicit'. This phrase embodies an internal contradiction between 'tolerant' and 'illicit'. It disrupts our feeling of a comfortable continuity with the past by pointing to something so paradoxical that it is hardly understandable. Foucault returns to us our own stories of the past, subtly refracted so that we are struck by the alienness of the familiar.

What can this phrase 'a tolerant familiarity with the illicit' mean? Before the seventeenth century there was a strong sense of the illicit in the domain of sexual practices, but at the same time an openness, a laxness in attitudes to talk about sex as well as the free display of bodies. The adulterer, the cuckold, the lusty wife, were all familiar stereotypes around which everyday conversation circulated freely. 'Knowing children', their 'innocence' intact, hung about amid the open laughter of adults. Bodies were displayed lavishly by low-cut dresses, codpieces, and so on, but without precipitating, or being seen to constitute, a general lasciviousness.

Foucault is making two points here: first, that there was a general ease, a tolerance, about sexual matters, or so the story goes; but second, and here Foucault edges into 'real' history, that there was a strong sense of the illicit in the sexual domain. The second point makes us reassess the first. It appears that the 'tolerance' extended only to the level of discourse, of the circulation of signs, without penetrating the not-so-secret-heart of the matter, the 'act' itself.

In the following paragraph, Foucault moves to the next stage of the story: from the mid-seventeenth-century to the modern period, of which the 'Victorian regime' is taken to be the paradigm—the era of the 'great repression'. He describes the latter in such lavish detail that only later do we remember, when he reminds us, that the account of the latter era is only a story we tell about our ancestors. Indeed, the story of the repression turns out to be a double fabrication (although a fabrication which is not totally a fiction) and Foucault's initial description of it, as if it were 'real history', doubly ironical. The first fabrication is that the period of repression was preceded by a period of enlightened innocence, a pre-seventeenth-century utopia and succeeded by a period of liberation (a point to which I shall return shortly). Foucault will argue that the function of this fabrication is to dramatise the repression as a divergence from some 'original' state of innocence to which we can perhaps return. (Rousseau's and Marx's myths of a pre-industrial, idyllic rural community both illustrate this dramatic theme.) The second fabrication is the repression itself, which Foucault describes as follows:

> Sexuality was carefully confined; it moved into the home . . . A single locus of sexuality was acknowledged, but it was a utilitarian and fertile one: the parents' bedroom. The rest had only to remain vague . . . if it [sterile behaviour] insisted on making itself too visible, it . . . would have to pay the penalty . . . It would be drawn out, denied, and reduced to silence. Not only did it not exist, it had no right to exist and would be made to disappear upon its least manifestation—whether in acts or in words . . . These are the characteristics of repression, which serve to distinguish it from the prohibitions maintained by penal law . . . repression operated as a sentence to disappear . . . an injunction to silence, an affirmation of nonexistence . . . an admission that there was nothing to say . . . to see . . . to know. (pp. 3–4)

The emphasis here is not so much on the confinement of practices but rather on the narrowing of the domain of the licit and a corresponding expansion of the category of the illicit. In other words, the repression operates not by physical prevention or force but rather by interventions into the normative framework and the discourses which frame it. Moreover, a new mechanism is used to maintain the boundary between the licit and the illicit: a discursive denial of the existence of the illicit, its silencing. By contrast, in the preceding period, the illicit was merely separated, its presence acknowledged, even celebrated, but circumscribed. The annual carnival can be seen as one element in the latter form of commerce with the illicit. The illicit was fully acknowledged, but restricted to a well-defined spatial and temporal location.[5]

In short, the scenario which characterises the great repression is an expansion of the domain of the illicit accompanied by its silencing. So the transvestite, the masturbating child, the homosexual are all denied, their location finessed as a 'demi-monde', a half-world on the fringes of society. They have no place of their own, even in opposition to proper society as its 'outside'.[6] (By contrast, the pre-seventeenth-century carnival had a well-defined public space and time of its own, outside, or underneath, the workaday world, where the world 'turned upside down'.) A homogenising, normalising logic applies every-where to every-thing, by the trick of defining any activities which fall 'outside' as 'no-where' and 'no-thing'. This is the rule of repression, brilliantly described by Foucault, but only, it seems, in order to question whether it ever took place.

Foucault goes on to show how this story of the repression can be expanded to incorporate Freud (p. 5). Freud did not, after all, liberate us. He allowed us to break the silence about sex, but only, it seems, by introducing a new private place in which to talk: 'that safest and most discrete of places, between the couch and discourse: yet another round of whispering on a bed'. Though the silence was broken, there was still no return to the storied public frankness and tolerance of the pre-seventeenth-century utopia.

At this point in his exposition, Foucault finally exposes his hand. At the bottom of p. 5, he launches a stinging attack on marxist histories:

> By placing the advent of the age of repression in the seventeenth century ... one adjusts it to coincide with the development of capitalism: it becomes an integral part of the bourgeois order. The minor chronicle of sex and its trials is transposed into the ceremonious history of the modes of production.

Marxist historians, it seems, agree to 'reify' the repression, but only because to do so reflects credit upon them by extending *their* story, that of economic determinism. On p. 7, Foucault points to other beneficiaries of the repressive hypothesis. We, all of us (Foucault's implied readers), benefit from the attractive picture of ourselves as progressive and enlightened because we understand and avoid the repressive practices of our immediate ancestors. Conservative forces in our society benefit too. Widespread acceptance of the story of repression enables a discourse of liberation which can be used as a popular political platform without threatening anyone's interests because it seeks a liberation from a non-existent repression. The new discourse of liberation deflects the gaze from the harsher realities which lie behind other, real repressions, and also fits well with the conservative structures of consumer capitalism: sexual liberation becomes a key element in the marketing of new commodities, becomes a commodity itself, which we buy through chemists, psychiatrists, and other officially sanctioned outlets.

Of course, pointing out the beneficiaries of the repressive hypothesis does not serve to discredit it. It only explains why the hypothesis would be popular even if there were no evidence for it. Foucault must do more if he is to criticise all those who speak the language of a past, and even present, sexual repression from which they seek liberation. He must cast doubt upon the *truth* of the repressive hypothesis. But what he says is this:

> The doubts I would like to oppose to the repressive hypothesis are
> *aimed less at showing it to be mistaken* than at putting it back
> within a general economy of discourse on sex in modern societies
> since the seventeenth century . . . my main concern will be to
> locate the forms of power . . . the discourses it [sex] permeates . . .
> how it penetrates and controls everyday pleasure—all this entailing
> effects that may be those of refusal, blockage, and invalidation, but
> also incitement and intensification: in short the 'polymorphous
> techniques of power' . . . to bring out the 'will to knowledge'. (p.
> 11, my emphasis)

Foucault's argument here presupposes certain historical processes, which he introduces in chapters 1 and 2 of section 2. He argues that a radical reconstitution of sexual activity began at the turn of the seventeenth century. The various marginalia—including talk about sex, gestures, displays, thoughts, and so on—all became central parts of the activity itself. The 'innocent' display of a breast, the wearing of a low-cut dress, became loaded with new meaning, not only as the circulation of signs of sexual potency but also as sexual acts. Revealing clothing became not merely a sign of wantonness, but a provocation; the distinction between the knowing innocent, the coquette, and the wanton became blurred.

The reconstitution of the domain of sexual activity by expanding it to incorporate its own margins was part of a general historical process to extend control over and discipline individual subjects. Any item of visible behaviour, any thought which could be extracted on the psychiatrist's couch or in the confessional in short, any aspect of the individual which could be surveyed, was subjected to a rigorous and continuous scrutiny, and either approved or marked for suppression. This process was legitimated in terms of a discourse in which every casual detail of the appearance of subjects, every fleeting thought, became a part or expression of their 'inner nature', and hence a proper object for attention by the surveyors who included the subjects themselves. The surveillance techniques were panoptic. Subjects were induced to survey themselves by the presence of an apparatus which enabled anonymous and invisible others to survey them.[7] In turn, the processes of surveillance confirmed the legitimating discourse; the public scrutiny of subjects served to reconstitute what was scrutinised as distinctively *theirs*, as expressions of their individual selves for which they were publicly held accountable.[8] In this way, subjects who were publicly constituted as 'individuals' in the innermost 'private' sections of their being made an entrance onto the stage of history.[9]

By incorporating discourse about sex as a 'core' part of an individual's sexual activities, it becomes a fit object for normalising scrutiny. Indeed, it moves to the very centre of ethical concern. Consequently, discourse about sex becomes illicit under the rule forbidding any 'non-productive' sexual activity which does not fit the model of fertile married coupling. Discourse about sex is labelled improper, except at special sites such as the confessional or the psychiatrist's couch, where it is sanctioned because it enables the processes of surveying sexual activity including, of course, the discourse itself.[10] This attempt to silence sexual discourses applies not only to discourse about traditional sexual activities but also to discourse about 'fringe activities', such as the discourses themselves. In other words, even discourse about discourse about sex is forbidden under the general rule against 'non-productive' sex. Not even the fact of a silence about sex can be recognised, because it too is banned as an item of conversation. In short, there is an attempt to cover all areas of sexual activity with a profound silence, so profound that it cannot recognise even itself. Foucault calls this complex process of disciplining sexual activities and the simultaneous attempt to silence discourse about sex 'the great repression'. It emerges as a special case of a more general process of the institution of systems of surveillance characteristic of the modern state.

So Foucault's final word seems to be that the hypothesis of the great repression is not *merely* a story which benefits its speakers in various ways. The repression, or at least the attempt to repress, was real after all, indeed continues up to the present despite our conception of ourselves as 'liberated' relative to our immediate ancestors.[11] Nevertheless, Foucault criticises the repressive hypothesis; not for its falsity (at least not in the first instance) but rather because it is incomplete and, in particular, fails to mention that the great repression brought in its wake whole new technologies for the *production* of sex. The exercise of repressive power in the modern context acted as an incitement to evade, and hence multiplied and displaced the activities which it sought to repress. This is not to say that sexual repression was ineffective. On the contrary, certain activities, such as the use of expletives in the domain of polite conversation, were effectively censored; but, in the process, new forms of sexual activity developed which evaded the repressors' gaze: ever more subtle innuendo evaded the ever more critical ear of the censorious. The repressors and the repressed were mutually implicated in the production of such new activities; the many-headed hydra became the figure for the new sexuality.

For example, consider the process of monitoring oneself for impure thoughts or actions. Such a technique for the repression of illicit sexual activity generates its own unique forms of transgression. The ambivalent satisfaction and disgust at uncovering yet another hidden impurity in oneself easily lapses into 'false pride' or even illicit masochism, and so becomes yet a further manifestation of a 'perverted' sexuality which must be rooted out, and so on. In short, every further penetration of one's own secret sexuality becomes yet a further manifestation of that secret which must be penetrated. As Foucault puts it, quoting Paolo Segneri's *L'instruction du penitent* (1695): 'This matter [sex] is similar to pitch, for, however one might handle it, even to cast it far from oneself, it sticks nonetheless, and always soils'.[12]

At a more prosaic level, the social worker and client, the psychiatrist and patient, act out their games of pursuit and retreat, of objectivity and concealment, of probing and seduction. Of course, there are real repressions here. The client learns to come to terms with him/herself, the patient cured, the pervert restrained/retrained. But these processes generate their own new perversions as the hunter and hunted warm to their mutual tasks: every seductive advance is met by a withdrawal, a retreat to silence or objectivity, every revelation deflected by the coy hint of further secrets. The patient limits the interrogator, repressing the invasive flow, in the same movement as the interrogator represses the patient by tearing away at the secret. Power and resistance are mutually implicated, limiting and also reinforcing each other, but without any net movement towards stasis:

> The power that lets itself be invaded by the pleasure it is pursuing; and opposite it, power asserting itself in the pleasure of showing off, scandalising and resisting. Capture and seduction, capture and

mutual reinfôrcement: parents and children, adults and adolescents, educators and students, doctors and patients, the psychiatrist with his hysteric and his perverts, all have played this game continually since the nineteenth century. These attractions, these evasions, these circular incitements have traced around bodies and sexes, not boundaries not to be crossed, but *perpetual spirals of power and pleasure*. (p. 45)

However, Foucault criticises the repressive hypothesis not only for its incompleteness, but also for its falsity. The repressive hypothesis and the corresponding thesis of a contemporary liberation imply that the same constitutive processes, including the panoptic system of individual surveillance which shaped our Victorian predecessors no longer hold sway today. Foucault opposes this implication. Hence the enigmatic title of section 1: 'We "Other Victorians" '; 'we' (all of us, Foucault as well as we, his readers) are implicated in the same constitutive processes which formed our immediate ancestors. So it seems that the story of a great repression and a contemporary liberation, with which we regale and seek to distance ourselves from parents and parents' parents, conceals an awful continuity. In other words, such a story plays the traditional 'ideological' role of concealing, providing a false representation, of the real mechanisms of constitution. But the story is constitutive as well, in the sense that it shapes its tellers in the image which it provides for them. For Foucault, as for Althusser, such stories are not mere 'ideological reflections' but also key elements in the constitutive processes by which subjects rework themselves.[13]

How can we oppose the power structure which Foucault describes? It is easy enough to envisage what opposition to an oppressive ruler means: civil disobedience, dissent, the violent overthrow of the state. But how is it possible to oppose the normalising influences which modern society imposes upon sexual being, when differences from and resistance to the norm are an integral part of what is opposed, when the system relies on the existence of such differences in order to feed its insatiable curiosity and infinite compassion? To resist, to defend differences, or even conceal them, simply provides more grist for the mill.

One strategy of opposition is to dismantle the whole panoptic system of surveillance, with its homogenising, normalising logic. But what is to replace it? Can we reverse history, and return to a simpler era, when the relations of persons with other persons and with themselves were not mediated by a system of public scrutiny? Surely the desire for such a return is pure nostalgia and ignores the real suffering and oppression which accompanied older ways of life. As Lévinas argues, in connection with another evil of modernity, money:

> Money allows us to envisage a justice of redemption to be substituted for the infernal or vicious circle of vengeance and pardon ... It is to be sure shocking to see in the quantification of man one of the essential conditions for justice. But can one conceive of a justice without quantity and without reparation?[14]

Money is repudiated for its alienating effects, for setting a measure on man, but that measure also has a saving power: it breaks the interminable cycle of injury and revenge by introducing a measure of justice and the possibility of reparation.

Foucault recommends the introduction of 'a tactical reversal of the various mechanisms of sexuality—to counter the grips of power with the claims of bodies, pleasures, and knowledges, in their multiplicity and their possibility of resistance' (p. 157). He looks forward to the day when

> in a different economy of bodies and pleasures, people will no longer quite understand how the ruses of sexuality, and the power that sustains its organisation, were able to subject us to that austere monarchy of sex, so that we became dedicated to the endless task of forcing its secret, of exacting the truest of confessions from a shadow.
> The irony of this deployment is in having us believe that our 'liberation' is in the balance. (p. 159)

But these comments leave open the practical question of how we ought to dismantle the normalising structures of modernity without losing its benefits: a welfare system which identifies and cares for those 'in need', a wages policy which sets and maintains a minimum wage, and so on.

Foucault leaves the answers to such questions unwritten. His text ignores the demands of the subject who wants to *know* what to do and who to be; indeed, he explicitly opposes such demands on the grounds that they are always and already implicated in the ruses of knowledge-power-desire by their desire to know, the desire for 'liberation'. He both criticises and excludes the Enlightenment subject who, in reply to questions of self-identity, looks for closed formulaic principles: 'Be happy!', 'Have faith!'. His new subjects must reconstruct themselves in the awareness that such principles, such 'liberations', are well lost, and so resist any 'austere monarchy' whether oppressive or liberating. The grounds for resistance will not lie in the spurious and dangerous generalities of grand theories of any sort, but rather in 'a different economy of bodies and pleasures'. Foucault's own writing is an expression of precisely such resistance: 'In the most hidden ground of his essence, man truly is only when in his way he is like the rose—without why'.[15]

NOTES

1 The opening quotation is from Reiner Schürman *Heidegger on Being and Acting: From Principles to Anarchy* Bloomington: Indiana University Press 1987.

2 Foucault's work has attracted many commentaries. Of these perhaps the most accessible is H. Dreyfus and P. Rabinow *Michel Foucault: Beyond Structuralism and Hermeneutics* Brighton: Harvester Press, 1982. Readers who wish to read Foucault at source may find it useful to start with M. Foucault *The History of Sexuality* vol. 1, transl. R. Hurley, Harmondsworth: Penguin, 1984, and the earlier work, M. Foucault *Discipline and Punish* transl. A. Sheridan, Harmondsworth: Penguin, 1985. A useful reference is M. Foucault *Power/Knowledge: Selected interviews and other writings 1972-1977* ed. C. Gordon, New York: Pantheon Books, 1980.

3 Foucault *The History of Sexuality* vol. 1, p. 1

4 For marxists, the economic domain is the background against which this 'seeing through' takes place. Foucault relies on a more general conception of 'historical truth' as the basis of a critique of discourse.

5 See P. Stallybrass and A. White *The Politics and Poetics of Transgression* London: Methuen, 1986.

6 Foucault acknowledges that the prostitute, the pimp and her client made a place for themselves where 'words and gestures, quietly authorised, could be exchanged ... at the going rate' *(History of Sexuality* p. 4). But such places, where illicit sexual activities 'could be reintegrated, if not in the circuits of production, at least in those of profit' (p. 4), were reluctantly sanctioned exceptions on the Victorian scene. 'Everywhere else, modern puritanism imposed its triple edict of taboo, nonexistence, and silence' (p. 5).

7 In other words, subjects monitored their own behaviour because of the possibility that they were being surveyed by others, who remained conveniently out of sight behind the apparatus of surveillance—see Foucault's *Discipline and Punish*. The ingenuity of such a system lies not only in the protection it affords those who are concealed behind the panopticon, but also in its cost-effectiveness (no one else needs to be watching if the subjects watch themselves).

8 In Lacanian terms, the constitutive effect arises because the panopticon comprises the voice of 'demand'—the inscrutable and (hence) insistent call of the 'Other'. That is, the possibility of my surveillance by an invisible other leads me to ask the question: 'What does he (that invisible other who even now may be watching me without my knowing) really want?'. So, I am led to construct a desire which the other has for me—'This is what he really wants'—which I then take as the desire which I have for myself. Even

if I resist what I construe as the desire of the Other, the constitutive effect takes a grip, in so far the desire of the Other sets the scene within which I define my own desire, and so too myself—see J. Lacan *Four Fundamental Concepts of Psychoanalysis* New York: Norton, 1981, chapters 17–19. Of course, the implicit assumption I am making here, that a psychodynamic mechanism of constitution can be projected into the social domain, needs further argument. For a sustained attempt to develop such an argument, see S. Zizek *The Sublime Object of Ideology* London: Verso, 1989. (Foucault, of course, never attempts to provide such a theory of constitutive effects, displaying an equal difference to Freudian, Lacanian, and marxist account of the subject.)

9 This account of the rise of individualism, in terms of the institutionalisation of panoptic systems of surveillance, is supplemented in the later volumes of Foucault's *History of Sexuality*. There Foucault argues that classical Greek and Roman techniques of 'care for the self' survive as elements of the constitutive processes which form the modern individual.

10 The semiotics of these special sites are constructed to minimise the danger which attends the free-speaking of sex. The one who confesses cannot see his/her confessor. So the normal power relations of speaker and hearer are reversed to the detriment of the speaker, that is, the speaker is disempowered in order to prepare speech for her/his dangerous message. The role of the psychiatrist's couch in the system of public surveillance (surveillance of the public) belies its appearance of privacy, an appearance which takes on the role of an ideology. Rather, the psychiatrist's couch functions as one of the 'devices of sexual saturation', along with the family and the school, where the boundary between public responsibility and the individual's right to privacy are negotiated to the invisible disadvantage of the latter. (See the discussion in *History of Sexuality* pp. 45–46.)

11 The *attempt* to repress may itself constitute an act of repression even if it does not achieve its target. In the same way learning to ride a bike may be an experience of learning even if the student never succeeds in cycling. In other words, 'repression', like 'learning', may not have a success grammar.

12 *History of Sexuality* p. 19

13 De Certeau, on the other hand, argues that the Victorian system of constitution, the panopticon, is no longer as effective in the modern (postmodern?) period; although it is not clear whether we would interpret such loss of effectiveness as the failure of the panopticon to continue its monopoly over the place of the Other, or (less radically) as the enhancement of subjects' resistance to what they construe as the desire of the Other—see M. De Certeau *The Practice of Everyday Life* Berkeley: University of California Press, 1984, pp. 179–80. The second alternative fits with Foucault's theme that, in the contemporary period, a further twist has been added to the spiral of power and resistance, and so the Victorian constitutive mechanism is substantially unchanged.

14 E. Lévinas *Philosophical Papers* transl. Alphonso Lingis, Dordrecht: Martinus Nijhoff, 1987

15 Martin Heidegger *Der Satz von Grund* Pfullingen: G. Neske, 1957, p. 73, quoted in Schürman *Heidegger on Being and Acting* p. 38

PART III
Social Context

Peter Cotton's chapter on Lacan is partly an account of his attempt to provide a context for his psychotherapeutic practice: what is happening when clients come to a psychotherapist to have themselves changed? To a certain extent, Lacan presents an account of how individuals find a place for themselves in language, though Cotton is critical of this picture because it does not give the wider historical narrative in which that individual is placed. Using Heidegger, Cotton reveals the dialogue between Lacan's theory of the split subject and the modern understanding of 'self-positing'. In this way, Cotton brings Lacan into the contemporary argument about the limits of constructivism: to what extent can the world be seen as the product of individual consciousness.

6 The cultural significance of Lacanian psychoanalysis

My original interest in Lacan was inspired by the prospect of a philosophically deeper reflection on the process of therapy than has hitherto seemed possible amid competing ideologies in the Anglo-American clinical context. The latter approaches have historically been dominated by technocratic conceptions of the process of therapy and overly constrained by positivist methodological prescriptions. This has doubtless been influenced by aspirations for credibility within the academy, as well as the preservation of disciplinary boundaries against the advances of other health professions. Alternative approaches, which have reactively embraced the 'humanistic' paradigm, have generally eschewed any rigorous reflection on the nature and process of psychotherapy. Be that as it may, I do not want to discuss further here the sociological dimension of recent psychotherapy theorising, but simply, by way of introduction, to point towards the constrictive nature of the Anglo-American ethos.

I was already familiar with the ultimately unsuccessful attempts of European existential clinicians such as Binswanger to reformulate psychoanalysis on the basis of categories derived from Heidegger's *Being and Time*, and expected that Lacan (who also counted Heidegger among his prominent philosophical influences) might offer a more satisfactory reinterpetation of psychoanalysis—particularly concerning the nature of the relations between the human self and presubjective levels of being, the domain which psychoanalysis theorises as the 'unconscious', and the role of language in therapy. Indeed, there can now be no doubt concerning the pre-eminence of Lacan's contribution to clinical psychoanalysis and his impact on psychotherapy theorising: the introduction of Lacanian psychoanalysis into the Anglo-American clinical community has opened a space in which it has become possible to think more deeply about psychotherapy.[1]

However, in examining Lacanian psychoanalysis from a more culturally oriented level of reflection, as I will attempt here, it becomes apparent, I want to suggest, that there are broader limitations to the whole psychoanalytic approach to thinking about persons. Accordingly, the fundamental problem for Lacan is his lack of adequate historical contextualisation of psychoanalysis; as I will attempt to show, in theorising the subject Lacan confounds the category of the individual with its contemporary historical form. A related issue is Lacan's overreliance on the metaphysics of language developed by structural linguists. Generally, this metaphysics is characterised by a formalisation of language at an abstracted level which allows it to be conceived as a self-referring symbolic network of words. The grounding of Lacanian psychoanalysis in this metaphysical determination has consequences which ramify throughout Lacanian theory. The later Lacan sought to temper some of these consequences through theoretical innovations in relation to conceptualising the domain outside language, the Lacanian 'Real', and the '*objet à* (the unobtainable object of desire which the Lacanian subject incessantly seeks). Nevertheless, Lacan was unable to extricate himself from a determination of being which, as I will argue, resulted in a problematic account of the constitution of the subject and of the ground of the self in the Lacanian symbolic unconscious.

Further, in reinterpreting Freudian notions ontologically, Lacan effectively pushes psychoanalysis onto terrain which has also been staked out by phenomenological thinkers—the most relevant for present purposes being Heidegger, although I will also briefly refer to Merleau-Ponty—who offer very different accounts of the constitution of the subject and its ontological grounding. I hope to show at a general level that a phenomenologically oriented analysis results in a more radical and historically appropriate interpretation of the 'psychoanalytic field'.

It should be obvious enough that psychoanalysis has historically evolved from a clinical theory into a philosophical anthropology, and with Lacan, into a fully fledged ontology and philosophy of culture. Such reformulations, notwithstanding theoretical disavowals, carry a representational schema of individual and social life which has a normative weighting that extends beyond the clinical domain into the conduct and framing of everyday life. Thus I want to claim that the cultural significance of Lacanian psychoanalysis ultimately turns on its framing of the possibilities for individual and social life under contemporary conditions. Hence my strategy here will be first to situate Lacan in relation to a phenomenological interpretation of modernity and then to examine how this contextualisation bears on the significance of psychotherapeutic practice in the contemporary setting.

I

The general thrust of Lacan's reformulation of Freudian psychoanalysis is well known. Lacan claims that structural linguistics provides the paradigm which can liberate psychoanalysis from nineteenth-century naturalism. Lacan thinks that Freud was already moving towards a linguistic framework but was limited by his philosophical milieu. In his early work in the 1940s, Lacan had already begun to reformulate psychoanalysis along existential-phenomenological lines largely relying on categories derived from Kojève's studies of Hegel and Heidegger's *Being and Time*. It was not until the early 1950s when Lacan read Lévi-Strauss that his linguistic reformulation of psychoanalysis flourished fully. His pursuit of the theoretical consequences of structural linguistics led Lacan to radically reconceptualise his earlier phenomenologically oriented formulations. Hence, in 1964, he referred to his Heideggerian philosophical interests as being 'only a propaedeutic reference'.[2]

What is important to grasp for present purposes is that in spite of his shift in theoretical orientation from phenomenology to structural linguistics and on to the difficult realms of mathematical formalism in the 1970s, Lacan remained tied to the structural linguistic paradigm. For Lacan, the field within which psychoanalysis operates is that of language and speech where language is taken to be coextensive with the domain of signifiers. Signifiers are defined by Lacan as the most elementary particles of language; they are 'ultimate differential elements'[3] which acquire meaning only in their mutual relations. Following Lévi-Strauss, Lacan terms the totality of signifiers the 'symbolic order'. The symbolic order qua domain of signifiers operates according to the 'laws of a closed order'[4] which function on the basis of 'the combinatory operation [of signifiers] functioning spontaneously, of itself, in a presubjective manner'.[5] In his seminar of 1954–55, Lacan seems to ground the symbolic order in something more fundamental which, following Heidegger, he terms 'Being'.[6] However, by 1960, he claims that there is nothing beyond the symbolic order that would ground it.[7] Lacan further elaborated his understanding of the self-subsistent nature of the symbolic order in his critique of the notion of Being in the *Encore seminar* of 1972–73.[8] Lacan thus insists on the independence and creative power of the symbolic order. The question we will be addressing then is, what sort of ontology is presupposed in Lacanian psychoanalysis and what is the phenomenological status of such an account?

By way of clarifying an interpretive position from which to begin to address these issues, I will begin by noting that it is difficult to find a place that is sufficiently distant to theorise Lacanian psychoanalysis adequately in relation to dominant framing assumptions about the nature of the self and the world. Psychoanalytic conceptualisations have nearly saturated cultural discourses, particularly in literature and art, and increasingly in social and political theorising. Moreover, psychoanalytic theorising is so close to the contemporary experience of individuality that it is difficult to separate them thematically. Indeed, another influential French thinker, Michel Foucault, eventually came to hold the view that his early work had been unwittingly enmeshed in psychoanalytic conceptualisations to such an extent that it had precluded him from adequately thematising the modern form of individuality. In *The Order of Things*,[9] Foucault exhibits a sympathy towards Lacanian psychoanalysis and accords it a privileged status in terms of its potential for 'contestation' with the analytic of finitude—the twisted conceptual strategies that the human sciences pass through in attempting to build theoretical edifices grounded in 'man'. For Foucault, man is a cultural construction—the peculiarly modern interpretation of human being as both subject and object of knowledge. However, in his later work, *The History of Sexuality* vol. 2,[10] Foucault informs us that a 'theoretical shift' was required in order to problematise the 'desiring individual'. Foucault now targets psychoanalysis and has Lacanian psychoanalysis in mind when referring to the 'man of desire' as a further phase in the cultural interpretation of human being as man. Foucault now thinks that psychoanalysis has played a central role in constituting the modern form of subjectivity. Psychoanalysis is henceforth seen by Foucault as an integral element in 'productive' power strategies which dominate individuals, in the mode of subjectifying and confessional practices, by constituting an inner subjective depth which only psychoanalysis is culturally legitimated to interpret. Hence the individual is 'subjected' by this domain of inwardness because the psychoanalytic injunction for individual life practice is that the unconscious must be endlessly monitored and interpreted according to psychoanalytic categories.

As far as it goes, Foucault's critique of psychoanalysis in its complicity and reciprocally constitutive relationship with the late modern form of subjectivity is illuminating. But Foucault's work subsequently moved in other directions and he did not pursue the development of an alternative account of the constitution of the subject which could serve as the basis for recontextualising psychoanalysis. Nevertheless, the point I am trying to highlight here is the need to characterise more specifically the central features of the contemporary cultural configuration and its correlative mode of personal formation. Only on this basis will it be possible to further clarify the ontological and cultural significance of Lacanian psychoanalysis. I will therefore briefly outline certain features of Heidegger's interpretation of modernity, not only because of his philosophical relevance for Lacan (and Foucault), but because Heidegger developed a phenomenological reflection on the constitution and structure of the human self within the context of a historical account of social forms.

I I

Heidegger's reading of history takes the form of a phenomenological analytic of the epochal social forms which have dominated the western tradition from the pre-Socratic Greeks to the present. It reveals a three-tiered process in the constitution of the phenomenal world: present entities, modes of presence and temporal coming-about or the event of presencing. To illustrate this, the present entities 'trees' have one mode of presence in the epochal constellation of the Middle Ages; coming to presence is grounded in God as the highest cause and beings have a specific rank in the hierarchical ordering of phenomena. 'Trees' have a different mode of presence in the modern world when they are constituted along with all other beings as the object world of human subjects. The third term, the event of presencing, is the temporal process of phenomena emerging into the openness of phenomenal appearance—and hence concrete signification—and their withdrawing or passing away. Heidegger thinks that the western tradition has never been able to think this third term, presencing qua presencing, for its own sake as the actual site of differentiation and upwelling (the temporal presencing-absencing) of world phenomena.[11] Instead, metaphysicians have always hypostacised presencing as an ultimate ground of entities. Nature, God and Substance[12] are some of the historical terms which have been used in the tradition to effectively contain the temporality of presencing and render it as static absolute ground and cause of entities.[13]

In this three-tiered process, human being constitutes a relational category between presencing and present entities, and serves as the locus of world disclosure, that is, as the historically constituted openness towards presencing within which entities show themselves. This openness towards presencing is constitutive of human being. Thus, in its ontological dimension, human being *is* as this presubjective and prevolitional world-spanning openness. Human being qua conscious ego is a derivative and always already situated historical mode of the more fundamental relatedness with presencing. This relation, as historically instituted by the epochal modes of presencing, casts the domain of what is possible for thinking and acting in any historical period. It is in this sense that the Heideggerian human self could be described as being 'decentred'. It is, moreover, relevant to note here that this account provided the philosophical paradigm which served as the point of departure for Lacan's retheorisation of the psychoanalytic 'decentred subject'.

Heidegger's 'epochal history of Being' reveals a series of successive transformations in the mode of relatedness between human being and world presencing. Here I will focus only on the modern epoch. Heidegger finds that the decisive event in the advent of modernity occurs in the early seventeenth century when human being progressively became 'that being upon which all that is is grounded as regards the manner of its being and its truth'.[14] Human self-consciousness henceforth became the subject par excellence and 'the relational centre of everything that is as such'.[15] This shift found its philosophical legitimation in Descartes whose central problematic was to create the metaphysical foundation for 'the freeing of man to a new freedom defined as a self-determination that is certain of itself'.[16] The general mode of personal formation which characterises modernity according to Heidegger is subjective individualism in its various phases, while engagement with the world progressively assumes the character of entities becoming objects at the disposal of the self-certain subject; 'the essence of subjectivism is objectivism insofar as for the subject everything turns into an object'.[17] For Heidegger, this mode of relatedness constitutes the grounding pattern of phenomenal interrelations and intelligibility in the modern epoch.

Lacan made use of Heidegger's history of the subject in linking the historical possibility of the psychoanalytic enterprise to 'the emergence of the Cartesian subject':[18] it is the unconscious of this type of subject, Lacan claims, that psychoanalysis works with. Heidegger's account of the trajectory of subjective individualism, as heralded by the Cartesian understanding of the subject, also philosophically

strengthened Lacan's arsenal in his infamous assaults on the pur-
ported ideological compromises of American psychoanalysis. Yet
there is an underlying tension in Lacan's theorising that becomes
apparent here, and which I now want briefly to indicate, by way of a
preliminary contextualisation of Lacanian psychoanalysis. The problem is that Lacan's theorisation tells us nothing about the historical
dimension of the subject. His ontological reinterpretation of
Freudian notions in terms of relations between the subject and language carries a claim to universality. As such, a question arises concerning the historicity of these relations: what is the status of the
Lacanian linguistically constituted subject prior to the advent of the
modern epoch and after, or whenever, modernity ends? Lacan
ignores this question. He locates the emergence of psychoanalysis
historically, but his theorisation of the subject seems to operate in a
historical vacuum. Unlike Heidegger, Lacan did not ground his thinking in a historical account of the relations between the category of
the individual and social forms. It is true that Lacan's theory of the
subject is posed in transhistorical terms, but this simply shifts the
weight of the problem onto historically changing modes of personal
formation and world-relatedness which Lacan does not account for.
The problematical nature of the Lacanian subject becomes further
apparent when situated in relation to Heidegger's discussion of late
modernity and the form of subjectivity manifested there.

Beyond the pluralisation discernible in every sphere of social life,
Heidegger finds that the most striking feature of the contemporary
period is the increasing ontological levelling out or homogenisation
of the totality of existent world phenomena. The self-assertive subject engages the world in a manner radically extended in time and
space and more efficaciously in the sense of its technologically
enhanced capacity to alter the very epochal fabric of our concrete
social existence, for example, biomedical technologies and environ-
mental engineering. Accordingly, Heidegger finds that the trajectory
of subjective individualism reaches its apogee in the contemporary
period as the dependence of human being on a particular mode of
relatedness to presencing is obscured, and all grounding referential
frames are increasingly interpreted as being entirely posited by the
human self. Heidegger's term for the final phase of the modern
experience of individuality is 'will-to-will': self-framing subjectivity.
But this unconditional self-framing is not something that is
volitionally adopted; it is the epochal imperative for individual existence into which persons are increasingly drawn in the late modern
world.

Contemporaneously, all entities increasingly come to presence in the mode of the 'constantly and simultaneously accessible', as the correlative object world of self-positing subjectivity. For example, the trend of modern communication and transport technologies is towards the 'abolition of all distances' in time and space[19] in which all entities and locations become evermore accessible, anywhere at any time. As such, these phenomena exemplify the general trend towards all world phenomena coming to presence only in so far as they enter the horizon of self-framing subjectivity, as grounded within the subjects' own self-positing projections. Heidegger terms this overall mode of phenomenal interconnectedness the Enframing or Technology *(Gestell)*: 'The totality of challenges that confront human being and presencing mutually so they may call each other to account reciprocally is the Enframing ... the Enframing fixes the pattern for our age'.[20] As such, this pattern radically abstracts human being and world entities from their mutual relatedness with temporal presencing, through the experience of self-framing and of world entities constituted in the mode of the constantly available.

Under these conditions, the relation between human being and language becomes a 'misrelation'. In the late modern world, Heidegger claims, 'language in general is worn out and used up'.[21] Hence the mode of language dominant in the Enframing tends to dissimulate and distort our relations with world phenomena. One implication of Heidegger's analysis which I will note here as a prelude to my later discussion on language, is that presencing qua Enframing, and its associated mode of language, are the conditions of possibility for the structural linguistic theorisation of language—the understanding of language which Lacan found so congenial with his project from the late 1950s onwards.

Paralleling Foucault's critique of psychoanalysis, Heidegger finds that psychology, and subsequently psychoanalysis, arise in the wake of the advent of the modern subject-object mode of relatedness where progressively, 'observation and teaching about the world change into a doctrine about man, into anthropology'.[22] Freudian psychoanalysis provided the grounding representational schema of individual and social life for a wilful subjectivity moving into a new phase beyond late nineteenth-century individualism. Freud redefined the limits of rationality but his critique remained firmly grounded within the normative horizon of post-Enlightenment critical rationality, the cognitive mode of engagement of the emergent self-framing subject. It could almost be said, in terms of Heidegger's epochal history of Being, that Freud obliquely theorised the ontological dimension of human being in certain elements of his conception of non-conscious subjective processes, that is, the Freudian unconscious.[23] But he did so in a manner which obscured the prevoluntary openness towards presencing and effectively subsumed it in terms that were consonant with the ascendant value system, thus becoming a domain potentially conquerable or at least containable by the emergent self-positing subject.

Psychotherapy and psychological practices in general do not fare well in Heidegger's interpretation of the present: 'When it comes to saving the essential nature of human being [that is, openness towards presencing], psychology—whether as such or in the form of psychotherapy—is helpless ... unless human being first comes to have a different fundamental relation to presencing'.[24] The question arising here is whether we should take this to include Lacan's reformulation of Freudian psychoanalysis. Or, more precisely: does Lacanian psychoanalysis subvert the complicity, suggested above, between classical psychoanalysis and the Enframing; does the Lacanian 'analytic praxis' provide a means of overcoming the machinations of the will-to-will and facilitate, at the level of individual practice, a 'different fundamental relation' with presencing?[25]

Lacan always resisted the characterisation of psychoanalysis as being reducible to a therapy for symptom amelioration; he harboured more far-reaching aspirations for its impact. Yet he was reluctant to pursue the implications of his formulations in this direction. In the 1954–55 seminar, a questioner suggests to Lacan that analysis amounts to a process of demystifying the ego and thus asks whether it follows that, after this has been achieved, 'All that is left is to wait and contemplate death'. Lacan's reply is: 'Why not?'[26] Elsewhere Lacan characterises analysis as the passage from 'empty speech' to 'full speech'.[27] This is to be understood in terms of the shift from communication dominated by the distorting 'imaginary' relations of the ego to the intersubjectively mediated use of language in which the subject becomes fully situated in the symbolic order.

During the 1960s Lacan progressively accented the radical division constitutive of the subject through its linguistic institution in the symbolic order; it is impossible to attain full self-possession at a symbolic level because the enactment of any unitary identity—which is the *raison d'être* of the phenomenal ego—is already mediated by the total network of signifiers. Accordingly, Lacan retained an emphasis on the process of analysis as one of breaking down the *méconnaissances* (misrecognitions, illusions) of the ego, but increasingly emphasised, as the end of this process, the recognition of the irrevocable nature of the division in the subject, and the necessity for the self to become reconciled to its own absolute determination by the symbolic order.[28]

Lacan's notion of the divided subject theorises what I have termed the self-framing mode of personal formation, and its principal constitutive tensions. But given my preliminary remarks on the historical dimension of Lacan's theorisation of the subject, the question remains whether he has sufficient grip on the category of the individual to illuminate adequately the possibilities for practice under contemporary conditions. In other words, restating the Heideggerian question posed earlier, is deconstructing the ego and learning to live with one's determination by the networks of signifiers an adequate response to the technological constellation of being?

III

How might Heideggerian phenomenology be helpful then in situating the cultural significance of Lacanian psychoanalysis? The first point to be made is that to the extent that Lacan remained indebted to structural linguistics for his understanding of language, psychoanalysis is complicit with the Enframing. The interpretation of language as a self-referring symbolic network of signifiers indicates more about the late modern world and its correlative mode of personal formation than it does about the ontological nature of language. Structural linguistics provides the metaphysics of language for the late modern technological age by hypostacising at a certain level of abstraction a particular historical mode of language. It is only in relation to this *a priori* determination of being that language can be interpreted as a closed order of signifiers. Moreover, the link between this conception of language and the Heideggerian analysis of self-framing subjectivity is obvious: the homogenised self-referring network of signifiers and the will-to-will share a common grounding in the Enframing as the late modern mode of presencing. This becomes further evident when the implications of Lacan's conception of the symbolic order are pursued in relation to his understanding of the 'unconscious', the self and the framing of individual practice.

Lacan theorises the ontological dimension of the self in terms of the (symbolic) unconscious: the 'Other of the subject'. The unconscious is elsewhere described as the 'transindividual' structure of language.[29] In later works, as Lacan sought to clarify further the theoretical foundations of psychoanalysis and assert its independence from philosophy and phenomenology, he shifted focus to the ground of the unconscious, which he now refers to as a 'gap' or a 'cut', and acknowledges that 'an ontological function' is at stake in the introduction of this concept.[30] He describes its 'elusive' functioning in terms of the 'locus of the signifier' where 'a stroke of the opening makes absence emerge'[31] and whose opening has a 'vanishing aspect' because it is also a 'closing up'.[32] Conceived in this manner, the ground of the unconscious is meant to be somehow primary and ontologically originary. One cannot but be reminded here of the later Heidegger's descriptions of the event of presencing, for example, as the 'giving' which always recedes because it 'withdraws itself and holds back'[33] in the presencing of phenomena. Yet the whole point of Heidegger's rethematisation of the 'Being question' after *Being and Time* in terms of the epochal history of presencing was the realisation that the event of presencing could not be reached by using the individual as a theoretical point of departure. Heidegger reached an impasse in *Being and Time* when the account of the cross-cultural structures characterising the existence of any human being came to be rethematised in relation to the historical status of the category of the individual. In other words, Heidegger found that beginning from a thematisation of the individual and then proceeding to the social, rather than starting from a historical account of social forms and contextualising the theorisation of the human self on this basis, undercut any claims to universality of the 'fundamental ontology' and prohibited adequate thematisation of presencing qua presencing.

The interpretive framework that I have been developing here, based on the later Heidegger, suggests that psychoanalytic categories have their conditions of possibility in the particular historical mode of relatedness between human being and presencing that characterises modernity. Freud grounded his theoretical edifice in a thematisation of a historically contingent form of the individual, and could only discuss sociality and theorise its origins in terms of early family relations, such as the dyadic mother–child relation, without being able to account for the historical casting of this relational form. Lacan's ontological reinterpretation of these Freudian terms as relations between the subject and language retains a similar problem because the Lacanian schema reifies particular historical forms of these relations and hence eliminates the possibility of change and historical shifts. Thus, psychoanalytic theorising, whether Freudian or Lacanian, cannot account for diachronic change in social forms. If as Heidegger would have us believe, the present is marked by a fundamental shift in the ordering and structure of the general social form, then the application of psychoanalytic conceptualisations to illuminate the social pluralisation and fundamental breakdowns of

the late twentieth century must be critically circumscribed. Phenomenological analysis suggests that any correlates of these broader
epochal shifts reflected at the level of individual existence cannot be
adequately subsumed within a psychoanalytic frame of reference.

How then are we to understand the Lacanian unconscious, this
'locus of opacity' which is 'ontological' and whose ground has an
'absolute, inaugural character'?[34] Further, how does the Lacanian
theorisation relate to the Heideggerian conception of the ontological
dimension of self as the constitutive relatedness to the revealing-
concealing movement of presencing? Phenomenologically, there is no
other way to make sense of Lacan's 'ontological function' than as an
attempt to theorise this same presubjective level of world
constitution.[35] But like Freud, for different reasons, Lacan is not able
to theorise it adequately because his conceptualisations are distorted
through a thematisation grounded in the categories of individual
psychology, even if ontologised, and further skewed by reliance on
the structural linguistic *a priori* determination of language. The
taken-for-granted self-subsistence of the symbolic order polarises the
presencing of world phenomena so that anything outside of linguistic
institution becomes 'impossible', that is, the Lacanian 'Real'.[36]

The later Lacan, in further developing the 'register' of existence
identified as the Real, refers to 'the encounter with the Real'[37] as the
limit point which always eludes psychoanalysis. Still later in the
Encore seminar of 1972–73, he refers to the 'empty space' which is
the area excluded by language which analytic discourse keeps 'bump-
ing up against'. However, as a consequence of his commitment to
structural linguistic metaphysics, Lacan continued to conceive language as a closed network of signifiers, and consequently as external
to the dimension of existence theorised in terms of the Real. Lacan
was therefore never able to grapple adequately with the relations
between language, the presencing of phenomena and their linguistic
encoding.

Lacan's notion of the *point de capiton*, the 'anchoring point' of
the signifying chain, does not modify this position in any fundamental sense. These points were never intended to be a 'pinning down' of
the chain of signifiers to any extra linguistic referent. Rather, the
concept refers to the contextualisation—or perhaps more accurately,
the 'punctuation', of meaning related to the points which mark the
beginning and end of a sentence. That is, because the meaning of any
sentence is only clarified at its end through being read backwards
after the sentence is completed, these points punctuate the retro-
active effect that signifiers have on those preceding them in the
signifying chain. Accordingly; Lacan claims that meaning inheres in

the relations between signifiers and their various associative contexts metonymically and metaphorically determined. Meaning, for Lacan, is never already in the world. Hence, signifiers are only related to entities of the same order, and nothing halts the 'incessant sliding of the signified under the signifier'.[38]

Heidegger, who begins his phenomenology of language by deconstructing the structural linguistic paradigm, is able to think more deeply into the domain which Lacan is forced to close off as the Real and its relation with the symbolic institution of phenomena. For Heidegger, language is always and already implicated in the temporal arising and showing forth of phenomena, as that 'waymaking' or lighting-tracing-out which subsequently lets words become bound to meaning within an epochal order of intelligibility. As Heidegger puts it, language already 'pervades and structures the openness ... which every appearance must seek out and every disappearance must leave behind, and in which every present or absent being must show, say, announce itself'.[39] This disclosive-showing character of language is not based on signs of any kind. Rather, the determination of language as a system of differences—as a domain of signifiers— already presupposes a prior disclosure within whose opening and for whose imperatives signifiers can appear as such.[40] Thus, for Heidegger, language qua language is the inherent meaningfulness, the 'gathering' of world phenomena which is prior to institution in verbal signs.

It follows from this phenomenological account of language that signs must ultimately always refer back to the presencing of a world. Without rehearsing in detail the relevant philosophical arguments here, I will simply note that any theorisation which does not suppose such a worldly grounding of language runs into insurmountable problems when pushed to account for the origins of language, of primal institution, and the historical development of language. Lacan's theorising cannot deal with these issues. Contrariwise, Heidegger's understanding of language can accommodate the self-referential dimension of the functioning of linguistic signs, which Lacan fixates upon. But, as I have argued, this aspect cannot be equated with the totality of language. It is, rather, the feature of language historically heightened under present conditions. Lacan's attempt to theorise the relation between the discursive and non-discursive from within the frame of the structural linguistics distorts it, and in confirming the almost exlusive concern of psychoanalysis with the symbolic order he is unable to say anything more about it.

The structural linguistic metaphysics of language also dictates the terms for Lacan's account of the irremediable splitting of the subject.

Lacan frequently discusses the instability of the unitary symbolic identity of the subject. The 'true' subject, as the 'subject of the unconscious', or the 'desiring subject', is in constant 'want of signifiers' to represent itself. This is because the subject of enunciation, the speaking 'I', can never coincide with the subject of the statement; the desiring subject is constitutively lacking. In other words, the speaking 'I' can never be fully captured in any first-person reference because of the logical impossibility of fully representing itself as the subject engaged in representing itself in language. Hence every utterance repeats the moment of irrevocable splitting. This is why Lacan can say that the 'I' of the speaker incessantly recedes or 'fades' under the chain of signifiers and is only sustained in the exercise of language. This account of the absolute splitting of the subject is, in terms of the interpretive perspective developed here, an artifact of Lacan's conception of language. The linguistically constituted splitting and bondage of the subject to the symbolic order is theoretical collateral of the late modern social form with its accompanying mode of personal formation. Elevated to a central position in Lacan's theorising, there is a resonance between the impossible symbolic identity of the subject in Lacanian psychoanalysis and the dilemma of the contemporary ideal of self-framing subjectivity whose very mode of existence requires suppression of its constitutive conditions. The Lacanian account, although ostensibly radically undermining the self-certain cogito, valorises a mode of being which ultimately cannot undercut the will-to-will. After all, for Lacan, the aim of analysis is to help the individual recognise her or his constitutive lack: that desire, as the fundamental dynamic of an individual existence, is ungraspable and can never be satisfied; that *jouissance* as the plenitude of being is forever foreclosed to the subject. The phenomenal self, as linguistically instituted and irreconcilably split, must learn to be relatively content as a decentred self forever roaming through the chains of signifiers—ontologically levelled out on one abstracted plane—obtaining only symbolic fulfilments. For the Lacanian subject, there are no practical possibilities for achieving social and political goals, however these may be conceived.

Phenomenologically, the psychoanalytic 'discovery' of the decentred self is not as radical as Lacan would have us believe. The Heideggerian analysis also suggests a subject that is decentred inasmuch as the 'ontological self' is not the self-conscious ego, but the prevoluntary openness towards presencing. This Heideggerian 'decentred subject' is not the origin of presencing and it is not a substantial entity. Rather, it is the dehiscence at the site of the disclosure of presencing and as such, it has its very being in the historically cast difference which opens up between presencing and world phenomena. In Lacan's theorising, this difference becomes an absolute and hypostasised split. Heidegger thinks that the phenomenal self is always and already situated by forces outside the reflexive powers of consciousness but nevertheless always has concrete possibilities open to it. In the contemporary setting, Heidegger claims, thinking and acting can learn to dissociate themselves from the technological constellation of presencing and 'heed the other destining', that is, potential for a post-Enframing mode of social existence, by learning to actively abide in the vicinity of the openness towards presencing. Phenomenologically, Lacanian psychoanalysis, with its emphasis on 'the scandalous lie' of any 'unifying unity of the human condition',[41] looks dangerously like an apologia for the contemporary experience of fragmentation characteristic of self-framing modes of living. What Lacan claims to be 'the essence of the Freudian discovery', namely the decentring of the self, or in Lacan's own words, 'the self's radical ex-centricity to itself',[42] is itself displaced by the need to move beyond the categories of individual psychology and the metaphysics of structural linguistics. The Heideggerian account of modernity suggests that Lacanian psychoanalysis frames the possibilities for individual practice in a manner that tends to reproduce the imperatives for individual and social life arising from the Enframing/Technological constellation of presencing.

More generally, the convergence of the phenomenological tradition and Lacanian psychoanalysis constitutes the beginning of what we might term, following Merleau-Ponty, an 'ontological psychology'. The Lacanian reworking of Freud has helped open the way by pushing psychoanalysis to its absolute limit point as the late modern form of theorising about the nature of persons. The direction foreshadowed by these developments also has implications for clinical practice and how we think about therapy and psychopathology, towards which we can only gesture here. We might have to consider that, at the end of modernity, the efficacy of the 'talking cure' per se may be waning as a historically appropriate way of helping people. At the very least, its wealth of clinical insights would have to be radically recontextualised and reframed.

Psychopathology, in a general clinical sense, would have to be reconceptualised along the lines of a distortion in the ontological dimension of self in which certain concrete relational modes are confounded or fused with the ontological openness, thereby generalising to an engagement with all phenomena.[43] Moreover, the phenomenological analysis of language and of the domain conceptualised in psychoanalysis under the rubric of the 'unconscious' suggests that the technique of psychotherapy cannot be constrained by the 'field of language and speech' as Lacan understands it—but this is an issue which must be pursued more thoroughly elsewhere.

If psychotherapy is to be appropriate to our time, a recasting of the 'psychoanalytic field' is required: a radical recontextualisation for which Lacan has already established a precedent in relation to Freudian psychoanalysis. The possibilities for reformulating psychoanalysis offered by recent phenomenological thinking may render psychotherapy more capable of contributing towards a historically appropriate response to the machinations of the Enframing.

NOTES

1 More of Lacan's work is becoming available as the later seminar volumes continue to be translated. Nonetheless, the best place to begin is still with the selection of papers translated from the original *Écrits* and published by Norton in 1977. *The Four Fundamental Concepts of Psychoanalysis* is also a central work.

2 J. Lacan *The Four Fundamental Concepts of Psychoanalysis* transl. A. Sheridan, New York: Norton, 1981, p. 18

3 J. Lacan *Écrits: A Selection* transl. A. Sheridan, London: Tavistock, 1977, p. 153

4 These laws, as originally identified by Jackobson, are the axes of combination and selection by which signifiers are related. They are used by Lacan to linguistically reconstitute Freud's two modes of unconscious operation, i.e., condensation and displacement, as metaphor and metonomy respectively—the two modes of relation in the Lacanian symbolic unconscious.

5 *Écrits* p. 21

6 In discussing Freud's notion of the 'navel of the dream', Lacan claims that '. . . there is a point which cannot be grasped in the phenomenon, the point where the relation of the subject to the symbolic surfaces. What I call Being is that last word . . .' (*The Seminar of Jacques Lacan* Book II, 1954–55, transl. S. Tomaselli, Cambridge: Cambridge University Press, 1988, p. 105).

7 In discussing the 'Other as locus of the signifier', Lacan goes on to state that 'there is no Other of the Other' (*Écrits* pp. 311, 316), i.e., there is nothing more primary or superordinate which would ground the symbolic order.

8 Lacan reiterates his argument that language cannot be grounded in anything beyond itself, e.g., as the 'language of Being'. Indeed, he now scoffs at any talk of Being, which he defines as something 'subsistent in itself, by itself, all alone'. This Being, Lacan claims, 'can only be supposed from certain words—individual, for example, or substance' (*Le Seminaire Livre XX, Encore* Paris: Seuil, 1975, pp. 107, 108). At this juncture, I will only

note that Lacan's critique of 'Being', which is, of course, directed against Heidegger, is misconceived. Heidegger never understood Being in the manner suggested by Lacan, i.e., as an hypostacised absolute ground of phenomena. In Heidegger's writings, Being (presencing) is always used in the infinitive to indicate the temporalising dimension of phenomena.

9 *The Order of Things* abridged transl., New York: Random House, 1973
10 *The History of Sexuality* vol. 2 transl. R. Hurley, New York: Pantheon, 1985
11 *On Time and Being* transl. J. Stambaugh, New York: Harper & Row, 1972
12 'The World as Picture' transl. W. Lovitt, in *The Question Concerning Technology* New York: Harper & Row, 1977
13 For my present purpose of situating Lacan, an element of distortion is risked in emphasising certain strands of Heidegger's interpretation of modernity, particularly in relation to the complex issues surrounding Heidegger's later reframing of the 'history of Being' in terms of the topology of presencing. Suffice to note here that presencing as event (*Ereignis*) does not function in Heidegger's writings as a transcendental signified or as any form of metatheoretical vantage point. Rather, the notion of event serves to indicate the limit point which Heidegger claims that thought approaches if it persists in thinking through the significant issues of an age deeply enough, and *experiencing* them in their epochal grounding. Heidegger understands the event as pointing towards the movement of the background of 'concealment' that always recedes behind what comes to presence in order for it to become present; it is the withdrawing of the 'hiddenness' in the opening up of an epochal constellation as a condition for phenomena attaining appearance and entering an order of intelligibility. The event of presencing thus surpasses, and can never be subsumed in, any cognitive schema.
14 'The World as Picture' p. 128
15 ibid. p. 128
16 ibid. p. 148
17 *Nietzsche* vol. 3, transl. J. Stambaugh, D. Krell, F. Capuzzi, San Francisco: Harper & Row, 1987, p. 211
18 *The Four Fundamental Concepts* p. 47
19 M. Heidegger 'The Thing' transl. A. Hofstader, in *Poetry, Language, Thought* New York: Harper & Row, 1975, p. 165
20 M. Heidegger *Identity and Difference* transl. J. Stambaugh, New York: Harper & Row, 1969, p. 63
21 M. Heidegger *An Introduction to Metaphysics* transl. R. Manheim, London: Yale University Press, 1959, p. 51
22 'The World as Picture' p. 133
23 As Lacan has pointed out, certain aspects of Freud's work on dreams and unconscious processes can be interpreted as approaching a thematisation of this dimension. To cite one example, of which Lacan (*The Seminar of Jacques Lacan* Book II, 1954–55. transl. S. Tomaselli, Cambridge: Cambridge University Press, 1988, pp. 105, 176–77) has developed a reading along these lines, Freud states that there is 'at least one spot in every dream at which it is unplumbable—a navel, as it were, that is its point of contact with the unknown' (*The Interpretation of Dreams* vol. 4, The Freud Pelican

Library, Harmondsworth: Penguin, 1980, p. 186, n.2). However, it is not Lacan's reading of Freud that is at issue in this paper, but rather, whether Lacan's reconstitution of psychoanalysis is any more capable of thinking the ontological dimension of human being.

24 M. Heidegger *What Is Called Thinking* transl. J. Grey, New York: Harper & Row, 1968, p. 89

25 I cannot discuss here Heidegger's understanding of the contemporary possibilities for practice as it would take us too far afield from the present focus and require a more detailed treatment than space permits. Suffice to note that Heidegger discusses the issue of a practical response to Technology (i.e., a different 'fundamental relation to presencing') in terms of 'thinking' which, in Heidegger's writings, designates an existential mode of engagement with the world which necessarily involves action. Heidegger claims that the phenomenological analytic of the epochal history of Being deconstructs the traditional theory and practice relationship, and opens up the possibility in our historical time of developing a mode of engagement with the world which cannot be situated in relation to any distinction between cognitive and practical activity—see Reiner Schürmann (*Heidegger on Being and Acting: From Principles to Anarchy* Bloomington: Indiana University Press, 1987) who has developed a lucid and comprehensive interpretation of this central but generally neglected dimension of Heidegger's work.

26 *The Seminar of Jacques Lacan* p. 214

27 *Écrits* pp. 41–43

28 e.g., *The Four Fundamental Concepts* p. 77

29 *Écrits* p. 49

30 *The Four Fundamental Concepts* pp. 29–30

31 ibid. p. 26

32 ibid. p. 31

33 *On Time and Being* pp. 9–10

34 *The Four Fundamental Concepts* 1981, p. 25

35 Indeed, W. Richardson ('Psychoanalysis and the Being Question' in J. Smith and W. Kerrigan (eds) *Psychiatry and the Humanities* vol. 6, New Haven: Yale University Press, 1983), in his sympathetic philosophical exploration of the Lacanian unconscious, finds that the only way to resolve some of the theoretical dilemmas associated with the Lacanian linguistic conception of the unconscious—for example, how to make sense of its ontological grounding and of the mode of being of the symbolic order—is to situate it in relation to this primal disclosive, unconcealing-concealing, dimension of existence. Similarly, Marc Richir ('The Phenomenological Status of the Lacanian Signifier' *Analysis*, No 1, 1989), in a remarkable development of Merleau-Ponty's thinking, shows that the phenomena analysed in psychoanalysis at the level of their linguistic encoding presuppose modes of interrelation that are irreducible to the metonymic and metaphoric linkages between signifiers. This level of emergent relations between the human self and world phenomena occurs prior to any symbolic institution. In a brilliant analysis of the Lacanian reading of Freud's Wolfman case (using Merleau-Ponty's 1964 Working Notes), Richir shows how an overemphasis on language—or rather, a particular metaphysics of

language—distorts the phenomena under investigation, and may carry important implications for clinical practice. Hence, Richir claims that we must now speak of the 'phenomenological unconscious' which is a dimension of world constitution that is ontologically prior to the symbolic unconscious as Lacan conceives it. Paul Ricoeur ('Image and Language in Psychoanalysis' in J. Smith *Psychiatry and the Humanities* vol. 3, New Haven: Yale University Press, 1978), in his critique of linguistic reformulations of psychoanalysis, also moves towards this ontological terrain with an analysis of the non-linguistic, but nevertheless semiotic and semantic domain of the image which he claims is obliterated in the overextension of the category of language to theorise this domain.

36 See *The Four Fundamental Concepts*
37 ibid. p. 153
38 *The Seminar of Jacques Lacan* p. 154
39 *On The Way To Language* transl. P. Hertz, New York: Harper & Row, 1971, p. 126
40 ibid. p. 123
41 'On the Structure of Inmixing as a Prerequisite to Any Subject Whatever' in R. Macksey & E. Donato (eds) *The Structuralist Controversy* Baltimore: Johns Hopkins University. Press, 1972, p. 190
42 *Écrits* p. 171
43 On this topic see Merleau-Ponty *The Phenomenology of Perception* trans. C. Smith, London: Routledge & Kegan Paul, 1962; *The Visible and the Invisible* transl. A. Lingis, Evanston: Northwestern University Press, 1968; M. Boss *Existential Foundations of Medicine and Psychology* transl. S. Conway and A. Cleaves, New York: Aronson, 1979.

Chris McAuliffe's chapter on Baudrillard attempts to show that there is more than one reading of his texts. He contrasts the tactical use of Baudrillard which governed its initial French reading with the more descriptive use that typified its reception in the Australian art world. Though McAuliffe favours the tactical nature of Baudrillard's texts, he is critical of the absence of any objectified field that would support such an operation. McAuliffe deals with the kinds of interpretation involved in translating Baudrillard into English. His own 'non-sexist' translations of Baudrillard provide an interesting case for considering the relationship between the original context of writing and that of its reception.

7 Jean Baudrillard

This paper can't be a commentary on Jean Baudrillard[1]: there is no singular Baudrillard, no static body of texts, no doctrinal unity against which all readings can be measured. In fact it's the multiplication of Baudrillard that interests me, the way that the vagaries of the translation of his texts and the historical, cultural and political context of their consumption generate a variety of authors. In particular I'm fascinated by the importance Baudrillard had and/or has for certain Australian artists and critics in the 1980s. But this fascination will produce an ambivalent and unresolved text. First, of course, I'll inevitably produce yet another Baudrillard, my own, so my thoughts participate in the multiplication in spite of any rhetorical claims to neutral observation of it. Second, I find myself thinking of the Australian consumption of Baudrillard in terms of fragmentation and misreading, as if there were a more accurate 'Baudrillard', one closer to the real author, one which I know better than his antipodean epigones. This response is encouraged by the ironic result of Baudrillard's dissemination: even as the author is multiplied he becomes something very finite and narrow, a proper name to be dropped into discourse, a set of quotations repeatedly cited.

Already, it seems, I've succeeded in reducing these multiple Baudrillards to just two—'theirs' and 'mine'. This is too simple, but I want to set up the opposition in order to signal my intention here. For a number of reasons, largely to do with the need of Australian artists and critics to theorise a postmodernism compatible with their interest in mass culture, reproducibility etc., Baudrillard was popularly consumed within the art scene as a writer who described the nature and operation of the mass-mediated present. I want to work through the development of his strategies more closely so that the nature of the Australian Baudrillard is more clear.

Jean Baudrillard, professor of sociology at the University of Paris X (Nanterre), translator of Brecht and Peter Weiss, author (from 1968) of some fifteen books and numerous articles, was effectively reduced to a series of articles published in art journals.[2] Baudrillard appeared, from late 1982, as the theorist of 'simulation' and 'hyperrealism'. Whatever the actual scope of his work he remains, for most readers, the author of a series of pithy, frequently cited quotations to the effect that there is no longer a substantive reality but rather only simulation: 'the generation by models of a real without origin or reality'.[3] 'A hyperreal henceforth sheltered from the imaginary, and from any distinction between the real and the imaginary, leaving room for the orbital recurrence of models and the simulated generation of difference.'[4] This Baudrillard is then used to underwrite critical and artistic practices circulating around issues of media, mass culture, reproducibility and 'postmodernity'.

The Baudrillard I want to oppose to this doesn't have the descriptive finality that his rhetoric suggests. What I want to argue is that concepts such as simulation and hyperrealism are developed during the course of an attempt by Baudrillard to formulate a practice which can begin to account for a social beyond the ken of orthodox Marxism and conventional sociology. In this sense Baudrillard's work is grounded in French history, especially the political and intellectual aftermath of May 1968: the recognition of inadequacies in Marxism and sociology, attempts to retool these disciplines, disillusionment with the Communist and Socialist parties, questioning of the epistemological bases of knowledge, and attempts to formulate new political strategies.

Baudrillard's work, then, describes a postmodern reality only insofar as

> The reality of Post-modernism is the reality of a tactic; the more widespread its application, the greater its claim to reality. The reality (a better term may be 'efficacy') of a tactic is not totalised or totalizing; for a tactic is not intended to survive its occasion.[5]

The problem in the Australian art context is that the strategic use of Baudrillard's work has been recognised but not its contingency. Furthermore, the inability to recognise the fully tactical nature of his work means that its dependence on specific contexts has been ignored, thus allowing literal transference and descriptive use of what is essentially a speculative discourse. As well, no real attempt has been made to determine the degree of efficacy his tactics have had, nor have Baudrillard's own efforts to totalise his tactics been queried. What follows, then, is an attempt to fill in some of the gaps so as to point toward ways or contexts in which Baudrillard's tactics may be useful in Australia.

Baudrillard's first two books—*The Object System* (1968) and *Consumer Society* (1970)—bear the hallmarks of a set of interests specific to France at this time: commodification, semiology, and the critical revision of marxist economism.[6] An interest in mass culture and the commodification of all aspects of existence coincides with the 'dethroning of economism in the aftermath of May 1968'.[7] Following Barthes, Baudrillard sought to substitute semiology—at this point the 'science' of signs—for orthodox Marxist political economy. Substitute is not the best word, since key conceptual elements from Marxism remain; use-value and exchange-value are thoroughly explored, just as a kind of Marxist scientism underlies his semiology. Baudrillard's procedure, like Barthes' in *Mythologies*, is that of the analyst standing outside and above his object, breaking it down into its constituent parts, displaying its mechanisms and their operation; in short, an alliance of Marxism and semiology under the banner of truth which demystifies its object.

But Baudrillard, like many of his peers, made it clear that Marxism in its classical form could no longer provide a thoroughgoing account of society. Consumer society could not adequately be explained in terms of use- and exchange-value. If advertising, for example, was no longer simply 'a discourse on the object, [but also] an object in itself',[8] if 'consumption . . . is an activity of the systematic manipulation of signs',[9] then the meanings of consumption were to be found in a semiology of consumption, not in a political economy of need and use: 'The social logic of consumption is not at all that of individual appropriation of the use value of goods and services . . . it is not a logic of satisfaction. It is a logic of the production and manipulation of social signifiers.'[10] If this is the case then the social doesn't have the concrete, causal, anthropoeconomic materiality that it used to, or rather, it still looks solid enough but it is all effect: 'Objects/ signs in their ideality are self-equivalent and can multiply themselves infinitely: they must in order to conceal, at any given moment, an absent reality. In the end it is because consumption is based on a lack that it is irrepressible.'[11] This is how Baudrillard ends his first book. The lack that propels consumption is not Marx's anthropological need but an absence of referents which sets signs adrift.

At this point it seems that the whole edifice of simulation—the idea that is Baudrillard for most art readers—was already in place in his first book. But I've deliberately translated the passage in such a way as to show the effect of a retrospective reading which seeks evidence for a Baudrillard it knows already. The verb *combler*, which I translated as 'conceal', can also mean 'fill up'. In this second translation the lack of the real might be momentary rather than terminal; that is, the real is always absent till a sign evokes it and brings it into presence. The ideality of the sign, then, is that classic semiotic manoeuvre: the curative sign restoring the real in a plenitude of meaning.

So there is no implosive circulation of signs yet. Indeed within a year of that first book, in 1969, Baudrillard wrote an article in which he made it clear that he thought there was still something behind the sign: the social in its most brutal form—class: 'Objects never exhaust themselves in the function they serve, and in this excess of presence they take on their signification of prestige. They no longer 'designate' the world, but rather the being and social rank of their possessor.'[12] Objects have a presence (possibly in and of themselves), indeed such an excess of presence that they signify not just use but the very ability to consume. Gadgets are a good example: electric toothbrushes, dishwashers etc. Exchange is no longer the circulation of surplus production, but of excess meaning; a kind of supplement to the object which takes on a life of its own, signifying itself as object of consumption and its consumer's class status. In this political economy of the sign, says Baudrillard, 'we would be dealing with (and this not only in the world of objects) a functional *simulacrum* (make-believe) [English in original], behind which objects would continue to enact their role as social discriminants [Baudrillard's emphasis]'.[13] '[The Object] is nothing but the different types of relations and significations that converge, contradict themselves, and twist around it; it is as such the hidden logic that not only arranges this bunch of relations, but directs the manifest discourse that overlies and occludes it.'[14]

If analysis is a matter of recognising the hard realities of power and class lurking behind the 'make-believe' of a 'functional simulacrum', then Baudrillard stands outside his object, looks through the surface, finds the real state of things behind it in depth. His object at this point is threefold: the simulacrum of the real, the hidden agenda which it conceals, and the inability of Marxist economism to even recognise this object much less theorise it. At this point his project is a *mélange* of Veblen, Barthes and those elements of Marxism not discredited after 1968. What is communicated in symbolic exchange is status and class; the effect, strategically and operationally, is one of power and acquiescence. Later, Baudrillard's project becomes, at least in part, a matter of determining the possibility of liberating acts within that very structure, but for many readers his work remains a description of the mass-mediated present.

So in the early 1970s Baudrillard mixes Marx and semiology: shifting the focus of Marx by attempting a semiology of the social in an age of consumption; shifting away from the formalism of semiology by attempting to ground it in the politics of class, power and everyday life. In 1972 and 1973, however, Baudrillard published two texts—For a Critique of the Political Economy of the Sign and The Mirror of Production—which signalled his increasing doubt in the possibility of Marxism and semiology accounting for the world. I want to point to something that's not given enough attention here. The critiques of political economy and semiology in these texts stem from a belief that neither can image the social adequately. The social that ends, and the real that is lost, however, belong to Marxism and semiology as paradigms. It is not the social or the real as an essence that have disappeared but species of theoretical and interpretive constructs.

The implications are threefold. First, Baudrillard's project is descriptive and analytic; he still seeks to map and account for the social. Second, his project describes the inadequacies of existing paradigms. A good deal of effort is devoted to the Oedipal project of demonstrating, if only rhetorically, the redundancy of these models. Third, his project is experimental; it seeks to formulate a methodology adequate to a new object. The social is a different thing and so must be theorised as such, likewise the sign. The knowing subject finds him or herself in a different position, perhaps not so knowing, not so distant from the object, but knowing all the same. If the project of the political economist or semiologist had previously been an empirical one—a matter of looking to see what is there—bolstered by the reality effect of an observer positioned beyond the object, surveying it with a panoptic gaze, Baudrillard's position is now a radically uneasy one. He looks to see what is *no longer* there, even as he attempts to describe what is there now (although this in turn may be an absence). And he still needs to formulate a reality effect of his own, even if this comes down to recognising that he can only rely on the devices of fiction or on such arbitrary devices as italics or bold type, the typographical equivalents of raising one's voice.

Baudrillard's stance in 1972–73 is somewhat different from that of his earlier texts. He now claimed that semiology did little more than describe the circulation and functioning of the sign, assuming that it could be pinned down and granted a kind of empirical status. The sign, in the conventional model, points to a referent, a slice of objective reality external to it but evoked by it: the sign brings the referent into presence. To use this model is, for Baudrillard, to fall back on a nineteenth-century idealism which breaks the operation down into a phenomenal level (the referent) and a conceptual one (the signifier). For him, however, the process could only be described as circular, not linear and causal: the real legitimates the sign, and the sign founds the real: '[The referent] is governed by the sign. It is carved out and projected as its function; its only reality is that which is ornamentally inscribed on the sign itself. In a profound sense, the referent is the reflection of the sign.'[15] '[The referent] does not constitute an autonomous concrete reality at all ... It is the world such as it is seen and interpreted through the sign.'[16]

Semiology, then, conceals a profound ambivalence in the sign. The sign marks the lack of a referent even as it constructs its plenitude. Reality becomes an alibi which shields the discipline from its own collapse:

> Thus, in a kind of flight in advance, the referent is drained of all its reality, becomes again a simulacrum, behind which, however, the tangible object immediately re-emerges. Thus, the articulation of the sign can gear down in infinite regress while continually re-inventing the real as its beyond and its consecration. At bottom, the sign is haunted by the nostalgia of transcending its own convention, its arbitrariness ... Thus it alludes to the real as its beyond and its abolition. But it can't jump outside of its own shadow: for it is the sign itself that produces and reproduces this real, which is only its horizon—not its transcendence. Reality is the phantasm by means of which the sign is indefinitely preserved from the symbolic deconstruction that haunts it.[17]

If there is no real against which to gauge the sign then there can be no history of the sign, no descriptive, narrative analysis of its operation. Since there is no beyond from which objective analysis can be conducted then it must be done from within that which it seeks to describe. I'm still using the word 'describe' even though I just said the normal conditions of description had been lost. This is because Baudrillard, in granting the sign a commodity form, begins to formulate a rhetoric which attempts to offer consumption as a kind of descriptive act. If the consumption of signs produces the real then an author's consumption of signs can substitute for description (and maintain a sort of beyond in refusing to accept the idealism which masks the production of the real). It is this strategy of analysis via embrace of the object which makes Baudrillard so appealing to artists working within a Pop art or popular cultural milieu in Australia.

Baudrillard's critique of Marx focuses on his analysis of production, rooted, he argues, in the classical models of production and labour, and of labour as an anthropological essence of humanity, thus reproducing and extending the very system which Marx purports to attack. In addition the Marxist model allows no place for symbolic exchange, for the analysis of the code. Instead, elements of a supposedly objective real are unquestioningly assigned values. For Baudrillard, in 1973, the logic of political economy is now that of the code:

> The signified and referent are now abolished to the sole profit of the play of signifiers, of a generalised formalisation where the code no longer refers back to any subjective or objective reality, but to its own logic ... The sign no longer designates anything at all. It approaches in truth its structural limit, which is to refer back only to other signs. All reality then becomes the place of semiological manipulation, of a structural simulation.[18]

But again, there still is a real, even if it is a pragmatic and operational one rather than being concrete and autonomous. (And later Baudrillard describes simulation as pragmatism pushed to its logical and extreme end.) So for me the important issue that he raises, and often neglects to pursue, is that of recognising an operational real and figuring out how to address it. There are times when Baudrillard spends too much time gleefully dancing on the graves of redundant paradigms and not enough filling the vacuum left by their demise. In *The Mirror of Production* his recognition of reality as an internalised semiological manipulation rather than directed reference to an external real leads him to conclude that a real is constituted in its totality at any given moment. There is no outside, no lack; 'Each person is totally there at each instant. Society is always totally there at each instant'.[19] This doesn't strike me as terribly helpful in the long run; it recognises the pragmatic generation of the real but avoids addressing its operationality in a puff of metaphysical smoke. Society is totally there, but as what? Man and women are totally there, but as what? Baudrillard's vicious semiological circle apparently describes the effect of a pragmatism without touching on the nuts and bolts of its operation.

I've almost reached the point which stands as the archetypal Baudrillard, at least in art circles: the theory of simulation, the logical consequence of the realisation that the sign refers not to a real but to itself. Interestingly enough it is abstract art that Baudrillard gives as one of the earliest concrete examples of simulation. In 1972 he wrote that in non-objective art, 'transcendence is abolished, the oeuvre becomes the original. Its meaning passes from the restitution of appearances to the act of inventing them'.[20] That is, the non-mimetic image does not transcend its materiality in order to refer to or to evoke a real beyond it. In 1976 he elaborated on this in an article on painting. He began the piece with a quotation on mechanical reproduction from Walter Benjamin but went on to make it clear that, if repetition has supplanted representation, the effect is more profound than Benjamin anticipated:

> Above all it is a matter of the collapse of reality into hyperrealism, into a painstaking reduplication of the real in preference to starting out from some other medium, be it reproductive, publicity, photographic: from medium to medium the real volatilises, it becomes an allegory of death, but it also reinforces itself by its very destruction, it becomes a proxy for the real, a fetishism of the lost object, no longer the object of representation, but an ecstasy of denial and of its own ritual extermination: the hyperreal.[21]

The rhetoric is vintage Baudrillard—seriality, circularity, death, loss, ecstasy, fetishism, masquerade—all turned toward a definition of a popular Baudrillardism, hyperrealism. But here, again, the transfer cannot be made without reference to the context of the text. Hyperrealism in this case does not refer to the phenomena which now serve as a description of the 'postmodern condition'; here Baudrillard refers to a specific style of painting known in Anglo-American culture as Photorealism; that is, the work of Duane Hanson, Richard Estes, the early Malcolm Morley. So Baudrillard isn't describing a state of the social so much as allegorising its condition through a mode of painting seen within a specifically French context. The status of the real has become even more attenuated then. If earlier the sign had preserved a phantasm of the real in order to conceal its instability, now the sign parades the evaporation of the real as referent in order to herald that which is more real than it, the signifier itself as the real. 'The very definition of the real is: that of which it is possible to give an equivalent reproduction . . . the real is not only that which can be reproduced, but that which is always already reproduced.'[22] Proposing the real as pure repetition is actually a means of escaping the crisis of representation, the loss of the referent. Escaping to what remains to be seen, Baudrillard himself wasn't too sure at this point. He suggested four possible consequences:

1 a deconstruction of the object into its constituent parts;
2 a game of perpetual redoubling, an internal evolution to the point of exhaustion;
3 the truly serial form of Warhol: neither paradigmatic nor syntagmatic, avoiding the simple tactic of internal redoubling by self-contiguity;
4 reaffirmation of the real in the minimal space between repetition and object; for example, the hyperrealist painting effaces itself before the real but the very difference, however minuscule, restores painting and object to their separate spheres.

Hence the much-vaunted implosion of the real into the hyperreal. There's a sense in which the whole process is framed as a parody of Hegel's *Aufhebung*. The real is surpassed, suppressed, yet maintained. Is the situation a case, asks Baudrillard, of 'the end of the real and of art in the total absorption of the one by the other?'. 'No,' he continues, 'hyperrealism is the apex of art and of the real through a respective exchange, at the level of the simulacrum, of the privileges and prejudices which found them both'.[23] Now as I've said, these remarks are all made in a discussion of painting. In 1978, two years later, Baudrillard extends this theory of simulation and hyperrealism to the social as a whole and states it more broadly, more aggressively, and in a more exaggerated form. In 'The Precession of Simulacra' Baudrillard overstates his case, and it's here that the prospect of his model serving as the basis for social analysis dims. I want to compare two statements, one from 'The Precession of Simulacra' and another from 'Simulacra and Science-Fiction' (1981).

Whereas representation tries to absorb simulation by interpreting it as false representation, simulation envelops the whole edifice of representation as itself a simulacrum. These would be the successive phases of the image:
—it is the reflection of a basic reality
—it masks and perverts a basic reality
—it masks the absence of a basic reality
—it bears no relation to any reality whatsoever; it is its pure simulacrum.[24]

This is probably the most frequently quoted slice of Baudrillard; it is what he has come to mean within art circles. I want to compare it to an alternative typology of the orders of simulacra.

—natural, naturalist simulacra, based on the image, imitation and counterfeit, harmonious, optimistic and aiming at the ideal restitution or the institution of nature with the image of God.

—productive, productivist simulacra based on energy, force, on their materialisation by the machine and the whole system of production.

—simulacra of the order of simulation, based on information, models, cybernetic games—on a total operationality, hyperreality aimed at total control.[25]

I think the difference between these two versions and the fact that only the first is available to non-French readers have a crucial impact on what Baudrillard means in the Australian context. The fact that the first is taken to be the definitive Baudrillard further compounds the problem. I find the second more tolerable because it doesn't get caught up in the seductive beauty of the model so completely. It recognises the mechanism of simulation—total operationality, pragmatism to the nth degree—and it recognises its end: 'total control'. The consequences of a general theory of simulation can be seen in both cases: the lack of differentiation between real and image which puts an end to representation as such; the impossibility of an image referring to something logically and chronologically prior to itself;[26] the constitution of modernity as the destruction of appearances and of postmodernity as the destruction of sense;[27] the simulacrum as 'an order which is neither of meaning nor of representation'.[28] The important difference lies in the fact that only the second recognises that simulation has a mechanism and an end which are synonymous. It recognises that 'simulacra are not a game played with signs: they imply social rapports and social power'.[29] It is this realisation that is missing from the art world's appropriation of Baudrillard. The patchy translation of Baudrillard, the desire for theory to come in ready-to-use chunks, and above all the absence of an understanding of the gradual development of the model within a set of historical and political circumstances demanding a newly theorised sociology all result in a simulation that is, for most consumers, a game played with signs. I realise that I'm using Baudrillard as an argument against himself here, but the confusion points to a tension in his later texts which has to be taken into account. The tension is between the descriptive aim of his texts—the declarative tone that affirms that this is how the present really is—and the polemical, rhetorical side, which tries to prove that analysis as it was once understood is no longer possible. So on the one hand simulacra point to real social power, yet on the other the social is something that revels in its own disappearance. The problem lies not only in the vagaries of translation but also in Baudrillard's delight in the consternation that the disappearance of the social generates among his peers. The tension in his project is summed up in this declaration of 1977:

The real is always that which it is, but there is no longer a sense in which to think it nor to reflect on it as such.[30]

From the late seventies, and especially in the eighties, Baudrillard shuttles between the assurance of his declarations and the equally assured conviction that nothing he says can be used to make sense of the world. The immediate implications of this tension for practice are that Baudrillard is often used in either a declarative, descriptive sense with no concern for operationality, or in a circular, gaming sense which recognises operationality but refuses to reflect on it. This is certainly the case within artistic discourse where Baudrillard is read as describing the actual state of things no matter how extreme his pronouncements. What is not realised is that his hyperbole and nihilism, his gaming tone, are a mannerist version of the Oedipal attacks on the edifice of Marxism and sociology which began after 1968. Baudrillard takes every opportunity to refuse dialectical analysis, to prove the inadequacy of his parent disciplines and epistemes; it is no longer a matter of analytic modes needing renovation, the present is now 'irreducible for any traditional theory and practice, even perhaps for any theory and practice at all'.[31] Baudrillard's project, initially a post-1968 renovation of social science, is, by the time he is popularised for the Australian art scene, one which circulates around a sense of radical loss: 'It is neither a question of some sort of dialectical critique of reality; rather it would seem to be the search within my object for a sense of disappearance, the disappearance both of the object and of its subject.'[32]

Hence Baudrillard's search for new critical strategies shows a predilection for fiction as evidence, for rhetorical paradox, and especially for the work of Borges. Fiction inverts the logic of dialectical analysis, the model precedes the reality it 'explains'. On the other hand, when Baudrillard resists the role of the rebellious child, he does see more positive avenues opening off from the failure of analysis and the loss of the real: 'in my opinion theory can have no status other than that of challenging the real'.[33] If the real is challenged, its exteriority and materiality refused, his task becomes more than that of mocking empirical knowledge and attempts to overcome the sense of powerlessness of a knowledge that no longer has a real that it can manipulate and change: 'theoretical concepts never offer an alternative reality ... In their most radical exercise, they make reality totter, they are a challenge to the real'.[34] Thus a new object is proposed along with a new subject position. The elusiveness of the real must not be halted but accelerated 'so as to make the system reveal itself more clearly', to 'reach a point beyond it'.[35] The project of demystification, which coloured his earliest works, resurfaces in a 'nihilistic' guise. The ploy suggests that the analyst does not pin down the object in order to dissect it but allows it to analyse itself by consuming it so eagerly that it reveals itself in an exhaustive frenzy: 'Theory is not grounded in acquired facts, but in events to come. Its value is not in the events that it prefigures. It does not act on consciousness, but directly on the course of things, from which it derives it energy.'[36] Hence the appeal of Baudrillard to artists with a Pop mentality. Analysis entails an active engagement with the object, demystification entails display through consumption. The problem in the Australian context is that the strategic complexity of Baudrillard's plan is ignored or unknown. Leaving aside the issue of the rectitude of the strategy it at least has to be acknowledged that his proposal goes beyond the superficial Pop/trash aesthetic touted by some of his antipodean epigones.

If theory is to affect the course of things there are, according to Baudrillard, three things that it must do (and these must be done at the level of the code, through a textual manipulation of the code). First, one must let the object take its course, consume it, accelerate it to its destiny, allow it to display itself. Second, the theorist must retain the position of analyst, even as s/he allows the object such latitude: 'One is compelled to produce meaning in the text, and one produces this meaning *as if* it arises from the system (even if in fact the system lacks meaning) in order precisely to play that meaning against the system itself as one reaches the end.'[37] Third, the system must be turned back against itself in a gesture of objective (subjectless) irony, adopting a position of provocation and analysis: 'There is a simultaneous requirement to give meaning to the text (analysis) and also to give an end to that meaning (provocation)'.[38]

This strategy allows Baudrillard to retain an analytical operation of sorts while refusing what he calls dialectical criticism—the knowing subject outside a static, bounded object. It allows him to perform a critical function from within his object. It allows him to critically modify the object without literally, causally acting upon it as materiality. This is the scenario in a nutshell. There is no objective presence to the world. The world is signed into existence not by reference to the real but to a code; there is no way to speak of the world sensibly. At this point one is left to engage in acts of consumption which show what is no longer really there. However, 'one has to recognise the reality of the illusion; one must play upon this illusion itself and the power it exerts'.[39] In recognising this one can choose 'to confront the world with the non-reality of its things' and this act would be a text which is not itself a simulation; it is not analysis as the projection of a simulated order onto an illusory real, it is a text which allows the illusion to be auto-descriptive. If one declares the end of the real one does so 'not in order to put a full stop to everything, but on the contrary, to make everything begin again'.[40] But begin as what? Perhaps as the same simulation, but again, it might begin momentarily and marginally as a speech which evades the simulatory model, which turns the model back onto itself and consequently steps outside its compass:

> The liberated being is not the one who stands in his/her ideal reality, in his/her ideal truth or transparence—the liberated being is the one who changes space, circulates, changes sex, clothes, morals according to fashion, and not according to morality, who changes opinion according to models of opinion and not according to conscience.[41]

The possibility of realising such a strategy and its efficacy are, of course, problematic, particularly given Baudrillard's tendency to take his own rhetoric at face value. My point is that the nature of Baudrillard's strategies have been given scant attention in Australia. Instead his work is taken as descriptive of a 'postmodern condition'. In trying to locate Baudrillard's work within a more specific epistemological context I'm not suggesting that it is wrong to read his texts within the domain of contemporary Australian artistic practice. Rather I'm suggesting that the conditions of transfer, and the regional Baudrillard that has been produced, should be more clearly understood.

NOTES

1 The following are suggested as a starting point that will give both a broad overview of Baudrillard's work and a sampling of key moments in his development: D. Kellner *Jean Baudrillard: From Marxism to Postmodernism and Beyond* Stanford: Stanford University Press, 1989; J. Baudrillard *For a Critique of the Political Economy of the Sign* [1972] St. Louis: Telos Press, 1981 and *Simulations* New York: Semiotext(e), 1983; M. Poster (ed.) *Jean Baudrillard: Selected Writings* Cambridge: Polity Press, 1988; P. Foss (ed.) *The Revenge of the Crystal: Selected Writings on the Modern Object and its Destiny*, transl. J. Pefanis, Sydney: Pluto Press, 1990.

2 The articles in question are: 'Hostage and Terror: The Impossible Exchange' *On the Beach* 1, Autumn, 1983, pp. 36–42, transl. Groupuscule Languistique [*sic*] de la Nouvelle Ville; 'The Precession of Simulacra' *Art & Text* 11, Spring, 1983, pp. 3–47, transl. Paul Foss and Paul Patton; *Simulations* [1976 and 1978] New York: Semiotext(e), 1983; *In the Shadow of the Silent Majorities* [1978] New York: Semiotext(e), 1983; *Forget Foucault* [1977] in *Theoretical Strategies* Sydney: Local Consumption, 1982, pp.

188–214 and New York: Semiotext(e), 1983; 'Mannerism in an Unmannered World' *On the Beach* 2, Winter, 1983, p. 30. To a lesser extent 'The Beaubourg Effect: Implosion and Deterrence' [1977] *October* 20, Spring, 1982. Two texts were already in translation: *The Mirror of Production* [1973], St Louis: Telos Press, 1975 and *For a Critique of the Political Economy of the Sign* [1972] transl. Charles Levin, Telos Press, 1981, but these were cited infrequently in an art context. In fact the selectivity of the consumption of Baudrillard is marked by the fact that it was really only the two articles in the latter text which dealt specifically with art which were cited.

Unless otherwise stated all translations are my own. Gender-specific nouns and verb cases have been eliminated where it is clear that the masculine has been used to refer to men and women; e.g *l'homme* is translated as 'being'. Wherever possible the original date of publication is given in square brackets.

3 'Precession of Simulacra' p. 3
4 ibid. p. 4
5 Rajagoplan Radhakrishan 'The Post-modern and the end of Logocentrism' *Boundary 2*, Fall, 1983, p. 57
6 J. Baudrillard *Le Système des Objets* Paris: Gallimard, 1968; and *La Société de Consommation* Paris: Denoel, 1970
7 Keith A. Reader *Intellectuals and the Left in France Since 1968* London: MacMillan, 1987, p. 13
8 *Le Système des Objets* pp. 229–230
9 ibid. p. 276
10 ibid. pp. 78–79
11 ibid. p. 283
12 J. Baudrillard 'La Morale des Objets: Fonction-signe et Logique de classe' *Communications* 13, 1969, p. 25; in *For a Critique* p. 32
13 'La Morale des Objets' p. 26
14 J. Baudrillard 'The Ideological Genesis of Needs' in *For a Critique* p. 63, transl. Levin
15 ibid. p. 150
16 ibid. p. 155
17 ibid. pp. 155–56, note 97
18 Baudrillard *The Mirror of Production* pp. 127–28
19 ibid. p.166
20 Baudrillard *For A Critique* p. 104, transl. Levin
21 J. Baudrillard 'La Réalité Dépasse l'Hyperréalisme' *Revue d'Esthetique* 1, 1976 pp. 138–39
22 ibid. p. 142
23 ibid. pp. 142–43
24 'Precession of Simulacra' p. 11
25 J. Baudrillard 'Simulacres et Science-fiction' in *Simulacres et Simulation* Paris: Galilée, 1981, p. 179
26 J. Baudrillard *The Evil Demon of Images* Sydney: Power Institute, 1984, p. 13
27 J. Baudrillard 'Sur le Nihilisme' in *Simulacres et Simulation* p. 231
28 *In the Shadow of the Silent Majorities* p. 54

29 ibid. p. 88
30 J. Baudrillard *La Gauche Divine; Chroniques des Anneés 1977-1984* Paris: Bernard Grasset, 1985, pp. 39-40
31 *In the Shadow of the Silent Majorities* p. 12
32 'America as Fiction: Jean Baudrillard Interviewed by Jacques Henric and Guy Scarpetta' transl. Nicholas Zurbrugg, Jean Baudrillard and Colin Crisp *Eyeline* 5, June, 1988, p. 24; originally published in *Art Press* (Paris) 103 (May) 1986, pp. 41-42
33 J. Baudrillard *Oublier Foucault* New York: Semiotext(e), 1983, p. 125
34 ibid.
35 Baudrillard *Cool Memories, 1980-85* Paris: Galilée, 1987, p. 288, entry dated October 1984
36 ibid.
37 *The Evil Demon of Images* p. 38
38 ibid. p. 39
39 ibid. p. 42
40 ibid.
41 J. Baudrillard *Amérique* Paris: Bernard Grasset, 1986, pp. 191-92

In his chapter on Lyotard, Julian Pefanis presents a political context for reading French theory which is characterised by debates about the legitimacy of the Soviet Union. This is the 'crisis of the metanarratives'. Pefanis discusses Lyotard's attack on the Freudian method, and his alternative which allows the object to 'be itself'. Similarly, the narrative workings of Marx are exposed in a speculation on his beard. In allying Lyotard's anti-militancy with Baudrillard's theory, Pefanis constructs a lineage of French theory which centres around Bataille.

8 Jean-François Lyotard

For some time now the thought of Jean-François Lyotard[1] has been receiving increased critical attention, and a degree of notoriety, in English-speaking cultural and art theoretical circles. He is being acknowledged as one of the major exponents of French post-structuralist theory, and has been engaged in a series of wide-ranging debates with German and Anglo-American criticism (Habermas, Wellmer, Rorty, Jameson, Eagleton, etc.). He is an extremely prolific and provocative thinker whose writings touch on virtually every area of interest in contemporary philosophy and theory. That Australian criticism shares these interests with its overseas counterparts is beyond doubt, and this fact alone provides sufficient justification for an examination of his work. But over and above these considerations, I think that his intellectual trajectory is relevant for those who have taken (or are tempted to take) the aesthetic turn of postmodernism. This is because it traces out, in a sometimes contradictory and confusing way, a general movement of great relevance to many thinkers. So rather than dealing with Lyotard's later writings (on the sublime, language games) I would like to focus on two points of this trajectory: his disengagement from marxism and Freudianism, and the aesthetic judgment he makes of both fields, in the context of an engagement with the post-structuralist pseudo-philosophy of writing.

> The enemy and accomplice of writing, its Big Brother (or rather its O'Brien), is language (*langue*), by which I mean not only the mother tongue, but the entire heritage of words, of the feats and works of what is called the literary culture. One writes against language, but necessarily with it. To say what it already knows

how to say is not writing. One wants to say what it does not
know how to say, and what it should be able to say. One violates
it, one seduces it, one introduces into it an idiom which it has not
known. But when that same desire to be able to say something
other than what had been already said has disappeared, and when
language is experienced as impenetrable and inert, rendering vain
all writing, then it is called Newspeak.[2]

The struggle against totalitarianism—against totalitarianisms—has
taken and takes many forms. The forms of this resistance are contingent on the techniques and forces deployed by the despotic
organisations, the Big Brothers. As political totalitarianism gives way
to complex new forms—technoscientific, commercial and linguistic
dominance of modes of life and everyday life—so new means of
combating them must be invented and thought. For Jean-François
Lyotard they are conditions that preclude a recourse to 'common
sense' and 'everyday language', since the events of the twentieth
century, for which 'Auschwitz' and 'Hiroshima' stand out as horrify-
ing beacons, have done something more than delay the progress of
emancipation set in train by the Enlightenment: they have clouded its
very ideals. For Lyotard it is not a case of abandoning the project of
Modernism—which is the charge levelled by Habermas against
him—but of the project having been liquidated by such events. The
postmodern (or postmodernity) is instituted and initiated by a new
species of historical crime, that of populicide. Lyotard is therefore
sceptical and resistant towards simplifications and simplifying slogans, resistant too towards the call and desire for the restoration of
sure values, by which he means the call to renew the project of
modernism (le project moderne). Slogans and simplifications are the
product of doctrine and the doctrinaire mind which is incapable, and
unwilling, to accept the singularity of the event which irrupts into
the order of fixed meaning. And yet the experience of art and writing
in modernism is anti-doctrinal, and, for Lyotard, has borne witness
to the irruption of meaning, to the irruption of the event, no matter
how lowly or earth-shattering. Thus Lyotard affirms writing which,
like Winston Smith's journal, bears witness to the infamy of bureaucratic Newspeak; he affirms that we must be guerillas of love against
the code of feelings: 'The labour of writing is akin to the work of
love, since it inscribes that trace of an initiatory event in language,
and thus offers to share it—and if not a share of knowledge, then a
share of the feeling which it can and must hold as communal'.[3] By
way of introduction, let us say that the problematic of writing is by
no means surpassed in Lyotard's theoretical propositions, and occup-

ies a central, even meta-critical position in his *oeuvre* (his Text). It is a position that might be described as an aesthetic which, in correlating the practices of art and 'writing' as resistance, defines his postmodernism as a direct continuation of the radical hypotheses of modernism.

Trained as a philosopher, Lyotard published his first book, *La Phénomenologie*, in 1954; it was not until 1971 that he published his next book, *Discours, Figure*, a version of his *doctorat d'état* on the subject of psychoanalysis and art. Since 1971 a very large number of books have been published over a range of theoretical concerns: art theory, psychoanalysis, philosophy, political and social theory, etc. A glance at the bibliography explains something here; in the seventeen years separating the first two books Lyotard's output is in the form of journal articles which are largely concerned with the Algerian struggle for independence from colonial rule (predominantly published in the review *Socialisme ou barbarie*); there are also several critical pieces in *L'Art vivant*, passing reference to marxist and psychoanalytic theory and a critique of Lévi-Straussian structuralism ('The Indians don't cook flowers'). But what seems to dominate in this period is the connection with *Socialisme ou barbarie*, a militant Trotskyist tendency which represented, along with other splinter groups, a tradition of non-PCF marxism and socialism in France. The group was committed to militancy and to workers' power and committed thus to theoretical practice defined as *praxis* philosophy. Lyotard wrote in this period, in a deeply productivist formula: 'Man is the work of his works'.

In this context, we can assert that the incredulity which Lyotard expresses towards the narrative of Marx, the emancipation of the subject of history and the historical accomplishment of socialism, was by no means so sublime as *The Postmodern Condition* might suggest. After two decades of praxis philosophy, Lyotard had, in a manner, lost his belief in the revolutionary program represented by *Socialisme ou barbarie*. Why?

This is a complex question, since in part we must consider Lyotard's militancy against the background of a countervailing tendency towards Nietzsche which had taken hold in contemporary philosophy, in the work of Foucault and Klossowski, but perhaps above all in the work of Deleuze. But as Lyotard himself avers, he is not above fashion; he is a philosopher *dans le vent*: phenomenology, praxis philosophy, Nietzscheanism, postmodernism, language games, desire theory—Lyotard is an opportunist, in a way a *promiscuous* thinker. Vincent Descombes, in *Modern French Philosophy*, argues that the militant Lyotard had availed himself of revolutionary theory that recounted the story of the contradiction of the mode of production, a contradiction which would lead either to war (or generalised fascism) or, through the mobilisation of latent revolutionary potential at the point of capital's crisis, to socialism. But, according to Descombes, Lyotard made two discoveries: first, that the truth which he thought himself to be speaking was in fact 'no more than a moral ideal ... It was therefore not *the truth* at all, but only the expression of a *desire for truth*'.[4] Second, that this collapse of the truth referent of revolutionary marxism was not of a movement in a philosophical game, but rather of an analysis of concrete historical conditions.

These discoveries can still, however, be generally related to the critique of Soviet state socialism generated by the *Socialisme ou barbarie* group. The major thrust of their analysis developed from a perception that the character of Stalinism was counterrevolutionary because it subverted that Bolshevik ideal of world socialism. It therefore followed that the communist parties in the west which took the Moscow line participated in the travesty. The perception was itself grounded in Cornelius Castoriadis' critical analysis of the mode of production in the putatively socialist economy of the USSR. In a complex argument, Castoriadis claimed to demonstrate that the socialist state, which acted as a concrete reference for socialists throughout the world, was in fact involved in a betrayal. Far from following Marx's formula for the equitable redistribution of the surplus, that state was, in effect, still involved in the construction of new forms of exploitation and domination in the sphere of political economy. The mechanism, and beneficiary, of this domination was, of course, the Stalinist bureaucracy. In Lyotard's terms this organisation incanted the narrative of emancipation while at the same time setting itself above the terms which it narrated, above the worker-citizens, above the Idea of the people from which it drew its legitimacy. Alas, was Althusser tragically correct in asserting the existence of ideology in socialism? This narrative of emancipation was ruthlessly enforced by a paranoiac organisation which could brook no counter-chant, no counter-narrative. The evidence of this, for Lyotard, was the historical suppression of what he had come to consider as a vital sphere of liberationist thought: art and literature.

For the disenchanted militant who had regarded theoretical practice as an important source of the critique of capitalist totality, it was an intolerable and hypocritical situation. For Lyotard it revealed a pious morality which inherited the Stalinist condemnation of art and literature as elitist practices. It was a morality which authorised a search for *salvation* and a *revenge* on the guilty. In this sense, the morality of militant marxism began to represent, for Lyotard, a thoroughly messianic religious metaphor. And as though this were not a bitter enough pill to swallow, it had to be washed down by the experience of the events of May 1968. These events, to a certain way of thinking, demonstrated the near-total failure of the organised militant left to participate in the ludic insurrection of the May Days. These organisations had failed to anticipate the sectors of contemporary society from which the rebellious urge would spring, and were unprepared for the sceno-dramatic effects of the critique of the spectacle. The situationists had been altogether closer to the mark. All in all, it was a very bad month for theoretical practice.

In 1964 Lyotard split with *Socialisme ou barbarie* on questions of theory and practice. This break, combined with a similar break from Freudian psychoanalysis, conspired to set Lyotard 'adrift', hence the title of the collection of essays of 1973: *Dérive à Partir de Marx et Freud* ('Adrift from Marx and Freud'). In this work Lyotard attempts to specify his relationship to the central practice and method of Marxist theory: the critique. Lyotard writes:

> If reason, which has been handed over to the air-conditioned totalitarianism of the very disputatious end of this century, is not to be relied upon, then its great tool, its very mainspring, its provision of infinite progress, its fertile negativity, its pains and toiling—that is, critique—should not be given any credit either.[5]

Reason, critique, power—they are all one to Lyotard. To criticise is to know better, and to fail to see that the critical relation maintains itself in the sphere of knowledge, and thus in the sphere of power. We have come across this critical crisis before, though not in identical terms, in the theory of the 'heterogeneous' as expounded by Bataille. His mystical *expérience* of thinking and exceeding thought at the same time, lurching at the edge of the abyss of *unreason* by activating the heterogeneous elements, stands outside the critical relation. The rejection of the critical relation is also found in Baudrillard's 'critique' of the 'critical mirror'—the reflection of Capital in marxism as the formal accomplishment of Identity in the thought of production.

When the name Lyotard becomes hitched up to an idea and an entire problematic of the postmodern (a term which avoids the specificity of postmodern*ity* or postmodern*ism*), it becomes possible to suggest that the 'crisis of the meta-narratives' can be read as a narration of Lyotard's own crisis with the meta-narratives of Freud and Marx, and a type of loss of political faith. The major text on postmodernism, *The Postmodern Condition*, is in many ways atypical in relation to Lyotard's other works. Published under commission from the Council of Universities of Quebec in 1979, and subtitled 'Report on Knowledge', the work is a sustained analysis, among other things, of the conditions of the legitimation of knowledge in contemporary science, a discourse thus following in the wake of the New Physics, fractals, catastrophe theory, etc. The source of legitimation for the authority of modern science is to be found in the philosophical metanarratives such as Kant's transcendental Idea of Freedom and the potential perfectibility of the rational, purposive subject of the Enlightenment, or in Hegel's culmination of world history and Marx's inversion of the same. The legitimacy of science is thus based on the deferred idea of the 'promised community'. Perhaps, above all others, it is this narrative of the promised community, which 'remains beyond reach like an horizon', which is fractured and liquidated by the irruption of the event—for which Auschwitz serves as such a potent sign. Reason in the service of the idea of humanity, in the service of its achievable end through history, stands crossed and doublecrossed at the threshold of *post-history* by the signs of its historical failure. Lyotard writes:

> The enthusiasm aroused by the French Revolution represented for
> Kant an eminent example of the unforeseen opportunities which
> such an event can grant us. In it he discovered the 'historical sign'
> of a moral disposition in humanity, and the index of a progress
> towards an ultimate goal for the species. If our feelings are not the
> same as Kant's it is because we are confronted by a multiplicity of
> historical signs—in which the names of Auschwitz and Kolyma,
> Budapest 1956 and such as it is, May '68, are evoked in their
> heterogeneity—each emphasising in their way the dispersion
> of ends and the decline of Ideas established in the Enlight-
> enment . . . [6]

The critique of semiological reason thus rejects the positivities of science and the Enlightenment ushered in by Kant's thought, and stand, before the collapse of their Ideas, in the condition of incredulity. One is in the postmodern if and when one is incredulous; to be reductive, to be incredulous is the condition of the postmodernist.

Lyotard got this condition from drifting—from philosophy to militancy into art via psychoanalysis, back through Wittgenstein on his way to the Greeks, ethics and paganism. Lyotard revels in a heterogeneous experience of knowledge—leading him to privilege the minor narratives which proliferate in the space of fallen idols, in the demise of transhistorical and transcendental values. Thus also a Nietzscheanism which reaches quite a fervour:

Here is a course of action: harden, worsen and accelerate decadence. Adopt the perspective of active nihilism, exceed the mere recognition—be it depressive or admiring—of the destruction of all values. Become more and more incredulous. Push decadence further still and accept, for instance, to destroy the belief in truth under all its forms.[7]

The situationist Raoul Vaneigem, in *The Revolution of Everyday Life*, repeats Nietzsche's description of the difference between active and passive nihilism. The passive nihilist believes simply in nothing, and passive nihilism is an overture to conformism. On the other hand the active nihilist 'criticises the causes of disintegration by speeding up the process. *Active nihilism is pre-revolutionary; passive nihilism is counter-revolutionary*. And most people waltz tragi-comically between the two'.[8] Lyotard would, in this sense, have to be classified as a pre-revolutionary thinker.

The game of drifting, however, dissimulated certain intensities in Lyotard's text, up to the point of their violent eruption in the work of 1974, *Économie Libidinale*—a work which Lyotard later describes as a scandal and devoid of dialectics in the Aristotelian sense of the term, 'because it is all rhetoric, working entirely at the level of persuasion'. What we have here, in the framework of a polemic and contestation, is a fusion of a Freudian theory of drives with a marxist political economy applied as an analytic of desire, a deconstruction of the intense sign lodged in the Text of Desire, or the desiring text. What I would like to do is to present, to re-present, an example of this operation, bearing in mind Lyotard's own caution in terms of the articulation of theses. While the libidinal economy is primarily concerned with texts, both as a theory of writing and as an analytic of texts, it can also be applied to any psychic apparatus, be it a written text or a work of art. In this respect, the 'libidinal economy' has an aesthetic dimension, and it evolved in Lyotard's thought (writing) in relation to his early studies of psychoanalysis and art.

Before we examine Marx's text, we need to turn briefly to Freud's general theory of the libido, which he characterises as the sexual drive. This meaning, as the sexual drive, is always present in Freud both in the noun and in the adjective 'libidinal'. However, there is a second sense expressed by the difference and *différance* of the terms libido and *libidinal relations*. For the child, as Freud tells us in *The*

119

Group Psychology and the Analysis of the Ego, the sexual drive is initially directed at one or the other parent. When eventually it becomes obvious to the child that this drive will lead nowhere, because it transgresses a fundamental prohibition of the symbolic code, then the child will produce affection instead. Libidinal thus refers to the affection which is produced in the inhibition of the sexual instincts. This theory is, however, more interesting in terms of its dysfunctional aspects, in terms of a theory of perversion in which the abnormal arrangement is one in which sexual attraction is expressed for those who are despised, while affection is reserved for those who are (merely) respected. This dysfunctional sense of the libidinal is, as I presently argue, of some consequence for Lyotard. In the same text, Freud remarks on the lack of criticism which is directed towards the loved one, and which he calls *idealisation*. This is particularly developed in terms of the psychoanalysis of the leader: the affection which the members of a group express towards a leader, and the feelings the leader has towards her or himself (the narcissistic type) or, more rarely, the feelings of the leader for the group (Jesus), are all likewise 'libidinal'.

Therefore when the analytic of desire is applied to the text of Marx, we can see that for the militant Lyotard there will be powerful effects to witness, particularly in terms of the dysfunctional psychoanalytic arrangement of libidinal relations. But we must not stop here without an idea of what animates the model, of what gives it a pretension to the economic. This is another Freudian notion found in the later theory of drives in the 'Metapsychological Essays'. For Lyotard these works, which introduced the death drive and the Nirvana principle, permitted Freud's theory of the libido 'to escape the thermodynamism and mechanism': his theory of the unconscious would avoid closing in on itself as a theoretical system. The Nirvana principle remained an expression of the undecidability of the dualism of the principle of life and the principle of death. 'Freud brilliantly said that the death drive works silently in the rumour of the Eros.'[9]

Once again, in order to grasp Lyotard's understanding of an economic psychical function, we need to refer to his work on psychoanalysis and art, which will demonstrate the way in which he plays the later Freud against the young Freud in the grip of the representational model. From this analysis will arise the replacement of the metaphor by the metonym, which is a legacy of the Saussurian theory of communication. The sign becomes, in Lyotard's analysis, a metonym of substitution, rather than a screen on which the subjective reference is simulated and dissimulated, and for which the sign serves as a substitute. This is very close to the way that Lyotard conceives exchange in the discourse of political economy; signification is deferred, interminable, 'meaning is never present in the flesh and blood', so that even the materiality of the sign is insignificant and not valuable in itself. Lyotard calls this process 'dematerialisation' and relates it to Adorno's work on serialism. Material in serialism is not valuable in itself, but in the relationship of one term to the next. The rejection of the Port-Royal semiology—a 'Platonism of the theory of ideas'—is thus related to the privilege of the 'libidinal relations' and libidinal economy over the libido and the theory of sexual drives, and to the condition of this 'dematerialisation'. This is a fundamentally modern phenomenon, and is the equivalent of capital in the realm of sensibility; it is the fragmentation and abstraction of signs and the fabrication of new ones. Recurrence and repetition are installed as basic traits within the system, and a new region, a 'pulsional strip', is colonised: the sculptural, political, erotic, linguistic, 'offering the libido new occasions for intensifications'.

The problem with Freud's aesthetic theory, explains Lyotard in the essay 'Psychoanalyse et peinture', was that Freud had privileged the subject of the work of art over its plastic support which, in the process of mimesis, is rendered transparent to the inaccessible scene behind it. In a further process, one discovers a latent content dissimulated in the object represented: the trace or silhouette of a form which is determinate in the painter's unconscious. Put simply, for Lyotard, Freud's schema made it impossible to analyse anything but the representational painting or work of art. Impossible therefore the analysis of the 'non-representational' painting in which the 'traditions of space of the Quattro-Cento tumbled into ruins' and in which the function of representation, so critical to Freud's theory, is rendered insignificant. To address the lacuna in Freud, Lyotard decides to read Freud against himself, by availing himself of the theory of drives and the libidinal economy. Lyotard expresses great hope for the new analytic arrangement, for it might free the object from a dubious psychoanalysis with an absent subject. It might also free aesthetic theory from its Platonism in which the object takes the form of a mimetic representation in the unconscious modelled as a screen or palimpsest and interpreted according to the law of the father and his symbolic code. The object, which is now free to be itself, can become the locus 'of libidinal operations engendering an inexhaustible polymorphy'. Lyotard muses that 'maybe the hypothesis should be extended to other objects, objects to produce and consume, ones to sing and to listen to, objects to love'.[10]

So it is in the context of a disengagement from Freud, from the Freud of the Leonardo studies at any rate, that the discussion can now turn to an aspect of the *Économie Libidinal*, itself a vast 'psychic arrangement' where Lyotard gives rein to his affections and disaffections. Specifically, I would like to turn to what for my purposes is the central piece of the work: 'The Desire named Marx'. Three reasons can be advanced for this: the essay gathers up, in an intensely rhetorical way, Lyotard's orientation in respect to Marx and the militant legacy he left behind; the essay serves to highlight Lyotard's own deconstructive practice of 'writing the impious' by applying the analytic of desire, with its *topoi* of repetition, delay and ambivalence, to the text of Marx, thereby giving form to his incredulity before the latter's meta-narration; the essay establishes Lyotard's negative relation to (actually another non-positive affirmation of) the thought of Jean Baudrillard.

The intention, declares Lyotard, is to 'take Marx as though he were an author' full of affects, to take 'his text as a folly and not as a theory', but without hate or devotion, to activate Marx's desire in the complex libidinal volume called his text. This desire is to be found not simply in the major theoretical works but equally in the margin 'at the edge of the continent', in notes and letters, in lapses and in the figures of repetition and delay in the machinery of theoretical analysis. To uncover this desire is also, in a sense, to uncover Lyotard's—the militant's—desire to unmask the process of capital, the desire to bring an end to its reign. It is additionally thus the desire of the idealist to bring about a harmony of people in nature, the love of people for others, of men for women and vice versa. All very well and proper, these desires, we might say; what is the problem? The problem is that these are not the only figures of desire at play in the militant idealist.

To awaken these closeted desires, Lyotard caresses a metonym borrowed from Bataille—Marx's beard—a partial object in a Lacanian sense, eroticised as a channel for the transference and counter-transference of libidinal energies, which is to say the object of a desire which is never directed towards the genital figure of *jouissance*, but toward a prolongation, through repetition and substitution, of an endless *deferral* of accomplishment.

The libidinal Marx is a polymorphous creature, a hermaphrodite with the 'huge head of a warlike and quarrelsome man of thought' set atop the soft feminine contours of a 'young Rhenish lover'. So it is a strange bi-sexed arrangement giving rise to a sort of ambivalence: the Old Man and the Young Woman, a monster in which femininity and virility exchange indiscernibly, 'thus putting a stop to the reassuring difference of the sexes'. Now the Young Woman Marx, who is called Alice (of Wonderland fame), is obfuscated by the perverse body of Capital because it simultaneously occasions in her a revulsion and a strange fascination. She is the Epicurean Marx, the Marx of the doctoral thesis, the aesthetic Marx. She claims a great love for this man of thought who offers to act as the Great Prosecutor of the crimes of Capital. He is 'assigned to the accusation of the perverts' and entrusted with the invention of a suitable lover, the proletariat, for the little Alice. The bi-sexed Marx is composed of stereotypes; the chaste young woman is a dreamer, dreaming of a reconciliation with her lover, while the man of thought is irascible and domineering. All the better to underline Lyotard's sentiment: this theoretical practice is really a very *male* thing, as it concerns metonym for the desire for Law, the desire of the patriarch (Abraham, Moses, Marx, Freud). And so Lyotard is led to say: theoretical practice is also about power, and not simply or not at all the power of the narrated proletariat, but the power which the militant assumes when the kid gloves are removed or, in default of the revolution, the power which is capitalised on behalf of the oppressed, which is also Alice's desire for something different and better. So the beard belongs to the Man of Law, the prosecutor of the crimes of Capital in the court of History. And yes, we agree, this is a great and important undertaking. Like a permanent crimes commission the lawyer works overtime in the British Museum, methodically considering every instantiation of Capital's infamy. And it is a very beautiful thing, this dossier on the accused, and it attests to an admirable force of intellect and invention, itself passably libidinal. But lodged in the massive machinery of theoretical elaboration is a figure of delay. For here there is an aesthetic figure which delays the appearance of the text on Capital: sentences become paragraphs, paragraphs become chapters in the cancerous process of theoretical articulation. The *non finito* of the text is evidence, for Lyotard, that what is being produced is a work of art, in this case a text. A psychic apparatus.

But Alice is restless, and she wonders why it takes so long for the intellectual head to produce the healthy body of socialism in the obstetrics of Capital. Why does the prosecutor take so long to sum up? What is it about theoretical discourse that makes it so interminable? It is, for Lyotard, because the result of this investment of time and grey matter can also be considered a *jouissance differée*, a *jouissance* of the same order as the *jouissance* of Capital—which is as a channel for libidinal intensities in its prostitutive arrangement. What is more, Capital will never give birth to the healthy infant of socialism because its body is barren, and Lyotard's (or is it Marx's?)

task is phenomenological, to bear witness to the stillbirth of socialism. Alice will be forever condemned to dream of that reconciliation, when she and her lover will meet in a different time and place.

Put another way, when something approaching the desired reality of the socialist body suddenly appeared on the scene, at the International of 1871, Marx was to write to his Russian translator, Danielson:

> It is doubtless useless to wait for the revision of the first chapter, as my time, for quite a time now, has been so taken up (and there is little prospect for amelioration) that I can no longer pursue my theoretical works. It is certain that one beautiful morning I will put a stop to it, but there are circumstances when one is morally obliged to be concerned with things much less attractive than study and theoretical research.

And Lyotard translates it into the libidinal: ' "Not very attractive", says the equivocal prosecutor, "your beautiful proletarian body, let us return our gaze once again to the unspeakable prostitute of capital . . ." '[11]

So here is the reason for the delay and the cause of Alice's unhappiness. The Old Man is cheating on her, besotted as he is by the object which he loves to hate. We could recall Alice's complaint: 'Jam yesterday, jam tomorrow, never jam today!' And this too can be translated: 'There was communism in the undivided social body of the "primitive", there will be a reunification of the alienated body in "advanced" communism, but today there is only alienation from the memory and the dream, the alienation which marks my body'. Everybody is going to pay for this, Alice with her eternal misery, the prosecutor in a mass of words, articulations and organised arguments—a theoretical torture with which he will martyr himself for Christ the proletariat whose suffering will be the price of its redemption.

Lyotard admits that it would be possible to use this religious metaphor in a critique of what is religious in Marx and in militancy: guilt, resentment and morality. But he argues that this reunified body, which is to act as the reference for the sacrifice of the martyrs or the agony of the proletariat, has never and will never exist. In any event, what would be the use of another critique, even were it to be an atheist one, and apart from the fact that there are already a hundred thousand of them? It would be to reinstall himself 'armed with bi-focal lenses, like some sort of Lilliput . . . on a small piece of the giant's posterior . . .'. Lyotard has something else in mind, 'something beyond religion and atheism, something like the Roman parody'. He would rather evoke the 'pagan' in all its heterogeneity, including the Clastrian idea of pagan society as primitive society, as society against the state, dialectically sublated in the parody: a joyous science of the Social . . .

So we come to the central propositions of the text: that all political economy is a libidinal economy, and the symbolic exchange is likewise a libidinal economy. Lyotard argues that, in referring to a 'prostitutive' arrangement of labour/capital, Marx presents a libidinal figure of the proletariat. Capital, the pimp, extracts value by alienating the erogenous zones of the prostitute, labour. In the analogy, the disconnected fragments of the body are linked to the fluid transformations and exchanges of intensities and signs in an endless account of 'incomings' and 'outgoings'. Lyotard understands that while such a regime gives rise to exploitation, to the domination and regulation of the body, it also involves another species of *jouissance*, to what might be called the *jouissance* of practical reason. For the ancient formula of Hegel—work or die, which means also to die or die *in* or *of* work—is refuted by Lyotard:

> And if one does *this* [work], if one becomes a slave of the machine, the machine of the machine, the screwer screwed by it, eight hours a day, twelve in the last century, is it because one is forced to do it, constrained because one clings to life? Death is not an alternative to *that*, it is part of it, it attests that there is a *jouissance* in it. The workless English did not become workers in order to survive, they were—buckle up slightly and spit on me later—delighted (*joui*) by the hysterical exhaustion, masochism, who knows, of *staying* in the mines, in the foundries and the workshops, in hell. They were delighted in and by the insane destruction of their inorganic body which was of course imposed on them, delighted by the decomposition of their personal identity which the peasant tradition had constructed for them, delighted by the dissolution of families and villages and delighted by the new monstrous anonymity of the suburbs and the pubs in the morning and evening.[12]

In the libidinal economy there is thus an affection for the prostitutive arrangement imposed by capital. To claim that this is perversity changes nothing, because, according to Lyotard, it was always so, and hence the impossibility of speaking of alienation; there never was and never will be a productive, artistic or poetic metamorphosis without the dissolution of the body. There will never be a resolution of the hermaphroditic text. Alienation itself springs out of the fantasy of such a body, a strange combination of the erotic, hygienic Greek body and the erotic, supernatural Christian body. For Lyotard, the militant's resentment (*ressentiment*) derives from a desire for the return of the whole body, the reunification of the (in)organic body of the earth with the body without organs of the socius and the body with organs of the worker. Nor is alienation related to castration, nor to the foreclosure of castration as Baudrillard's symbolic exchange might have it. Castration has no part in the fundamental schema which, as Baudrillard himself will point out, is deeply economistic, deeply exchangist. The fear of alienation is not the fear of loss, but the fear of not being able to give, of not being able to enter into the flux of exchanges and the investment of energies, even the deferred, strange and partial *jouissance* of partial bodies: the autonomisation and metamorphoses of the fragmented body in production, their investment in the labour-time of the system. The metaphor of the unified body, whether in mythic communism of the 'pre-economy' is ultimately religious, since 'the only way of not being alienated since Hegel, and no doubt Jesus, is to be God'.

From our point of view 'The Desire Named Marx' is also a significant text because it is one of the few places in contemporary French literature where Baudrillard's thought is examined in any detail, and it is especially significant in that it occurs in the context of Lyotard's rendezvous with desire in Marx. Lyotard describes his relationship with Baudrillard as co-polarised and synchronised, but claims that the latter's thought is burdened by theoretical and critical hypotheses—even though Baudrillard's denunciation of the critical and the theoretical (in *The Mirror of Production*) are made in formulae which Lyotard would joyfully countersign. The problem for Lyotard is that Baudrillard still aims at the true when he reproaches marxism for censuring and debarring social relationships commanded by the symbolic exchange—relationships centred on the exhaustion of libidinal energies of love and death. Lyotard's critique amounts to a sort of critique of Baudrillard's anthropological critique. For Lyotard it is a fantasy to imagine a society without political economy and without the unconscious, or to imagine that political economy or the unconscious appeared *sponte sua*, from thin air and then to be imposed on the social body which had not known them; or to imagine that political economy was not present 'in filigree, in embryo' in archaic society. Just like the commodity in Marx, Bataille's potlach is emphatically as much a figure of order as the former: they both compose the semiotic surface of the social. Mauss understood this in terms of the interest which accrues in the cycles of the exchange of gifts. That the symbolic exchange is charged with powerful effect changes nothing for, as Lyotard tells us, to have a 'lack' is the same thing as having any other sort of 'have'. It is a similar fantasy, for Lyotard, as believing there is a human nature which is good to the degree that it is rebellious, the same dream as Plato's when he sought 'a source for his Atlantic Utopia among the ancient savages of Egypt'; the same dream as Marx's when he invents the proletariat as the negation of negation and the place of the absence of contradiction and alienation; the same as Baudrillard's when he discovers, positively, that subversive reference in today's 'marginals'. The dream is one of a 'non-alienated region' which would be able to escape the law of Capital. But there is no 'region' which can escape the regimes of power, 'regime and region, sign and apparatus'. To have faith in one recommences religion, and this will assure us of being desperate: 'Perhaps', writes Lyotard, 'in terms of politics, our desire is to be, and always remain, desperate . . . ?'

Let us conclude here on a note of the co-polarity in the thought of the two postmodernists. It's possible, if in the circumstances parodic, to call this thought dialectically opposed, a dialectic in, and of, postmodernism. Lyotard's ironic affirmation of the system of production and exchange which champions the inventive moves it allows in technology, science and the realm of sensibility, the potentiality of artistic and linguistic expression in cultures of the *avant-garde* is momentarily mirrored in Baudrillard's denunciation of the same, in his fascination with the perverse polymorphy of signification. But in spite of their rejection of critique and dialectical thought, they carry on the critique by other means. The continuity of their thought on writing—instituted by Bataille—can be instructively compared. In *Just Gaming*, Lyotard remarks: 'The difference between what I write and poetry and literature is that, in principle, what I write is not fiction. But I do wonder more and more: is there a real difference between a theory and a fiction? After all, don't we have the right to present theoretical statements under the form of fictions? Not *under* the form, but *in* the form'.[13] In an interview on the publication of the book *L'Amérique*, Baudrillard says something similar:

> I do not really think of myself as a philosopher. Criticism (*critique*) has come to me through a movement of radicality which has a poetic, as opposed to philosophical, origin. It is not a function of distantiation or I know not what dialectical critique of phenomena: it would rather be the attempt to seek in the object and the subject itself at the same time.[14]

In proposing a relationship between theory and fiction—between philosophy and poetry—the postmodernists have underlined, in a way, the continuity of their thought and writing with the thought and writing of Bataille. They are simultaneously witnesses (no doubt phenomenological) and participants in an aesthetic movement, instituted by the critical surrealism of Bataille, which introduces into the philosophically serious the figures of the game: an indeterminacy and a disintegration of the certainties and positivities of so-called theoretical thought—radically questioning the function of criticism and the role of writing and art and the very position of the other in western thought.

NOTES

1 Since this chapter was written there has been considerable activity in the English language publication of Lyotard's writings, most notably of *The Differend* (transl. George Van Der Abbeele, Manchester: Manchester University Press, 1988) and *The Lyotard Reader* (ed. Andrew Benjamin, Oxford: Basil Blackwell, 1989). The latter work contains a comprehensive select bibliography of English translations of Lyotard's writing. Of course, his thought has already attracted considerable attention in the global sphere of theory. At random one might refer to the French publication *L'Arc* 64, 1976 devoted to an analysis of his thought, and in particular *Économie libidinale*; or else one might turn to *Postmodernism* in the ICA Document Series, a work based on a two-day conference held in 1985 largely in response to the publication of Lyotard's *The Postmodern Condition*. Alternatively one might turn to Stuart Sim's 'Lyotard and the politics of anti-foundationalism' in *Radical Philosophy* 44, Autumn 1986; or to Peter Daws 'Adorno, post-structuralism and the critique of identity' *New Left Review* 157, May/June, 1986, or to Albrecht Wellmer 'On the dialectic of modernism and postmodernism' *Praxis International* 4, 4, 1985— though this list by no means exhausts the critical reception of Lyotard's thought. This chapter is a modified version of an essay in my *Heterology and the Postmodern: Bataille, Baudrillard and Lyotard* Sydney: Allen & Unwin, 1991.
2 J.-F. Lyotard *Le Postmoderne expliqué aux enfants* Paris: Galilée, 1986, pp. 139–40
3 ibid. p. 150
4 Vincent Descombes *Modern French Philosophy* transl. L. Scott-Fox and J. M. Harding, Cambridge: Cambridge University Press, 1980, p. 181
5 J.-F. Lyotard *Driftworks* ed. R. McKeon, New York: Semiotext(e), 1984, p. 11
6 J.-F. Lyotard and Jacob Rogozinski 'La Police de la Pensée', *L'Autre Journal* 10, December 1985, p. 34
7 *Driftworks* endnotes
8 Raoul Vaneigem *The Revolution of Everyday Life* transl. Donald Nicholson-Smith, London: Left Bank Books and Rebel Press, 1983, p. 136

9 J.-F. Lyotard *Économie libidinale* Paris: Minuit, 1974, p. 27

10 J.-F. Lyotard 'Psychanalyse et la peinture' *Encylopedia Universalis* 1972, p. 747

11 *Économie libidinale* p. 122

12 ibid. p. 136

13 J.-F. Lyotard *Just Gaming* transl. W. Godzich, Manchester: Manchester University Press, 1985, p. 5

14 Jean Baudrillard, interview with G. Scarpetta in *Art Press* 103, May, 1986, pp. 40–42

Clare O'Farrell's reading of Bourdieu takes the novel path of using information about the author's biography to interpret his position within the French intellectual scene. This is a 'double reading' where Bourdieu is subject to a 'Bourdieu' style of analysis. In doing this O'Farrell points to the inability of Bourdieu's theory to mark the limits of its use.

9 Pierre Bourdieu
Sociology as a 'world vision'

Since the late 1950s, the French sociologist Pierre Bourdieu[1] has been steadily producing a body of work remarkable not only for its immense volume but also for the enormous range of subject areas and disciplines it covers. Yet it is only in recent years that Anglo-Saxon audiences, beyond a fairly restricted circle of educationalists, have begun to pay close attention to him. Bourdieu's now classic work *Distinction: A Social Critique of the Judgement of Taste*, translated into English in 1984, and his more recently translated *Homo Academicus* have both contributed to this broadening of interest. In France itself, the growth of his popularity is more than evident in the results of two surveys listing the most popular and influential intellectuals in France. In the first survey conducted in 1981, Bourdieu was number 36 on the list. In February 1989, a second survey registered his meteoric rise to fifth place.[2]

Yet Bourdieu still remains relatively unfamiliar to English-speaking readers, particularly when one considers the reception of the work of certain other of his contemporaries such as Foucault, Barthes, Lacan, Althusser and Derrida. This chapter will therefore seek to provide a general introduction to Bourdieu's work and its context rather than attempting to build a magnificent and elegant edifice of theory.[3]

One cannot insist too often that the consideration of historical and social context is essential in any discussion of French thought (or any other thought for that matter). Unfortunately what often happens in the English language discussion of French ideas is that the original historical, intellectual, social and political context is largely ignored. If more attention was paid to this context, some of the ideas imported from France would lose their mystic aura of mysterious and delphic dogmas, avatars of the pure realm of disinterested thought. Once that context is understood it becomes much easier to see how certain ideas can be modified and put to use in a totally different environment.[4] If such an approach needs further explanation, or better still the respectable seal of authority, one can do no better than refer to the projects of the 'New Historians', the work of Michel Foucault and Pierre Bourdieu himself who both treat ideas as so many historical and social *practices* and *events* which operate within a system of complex historical and quite material relations, none of which can be reduced to each other.[5] This is precisely the kind of approach Bourdieu takes in his recent book on Heidegger:

> The most suitable analysis is constructed on a double refusal: it rejects the pretention of the philosophical text to absolute autonomy and the correlating refusal of any external reference, and it also rejects the direct reduction of the text to the most general conditions of its production.[6]

Thus one must abandon the traditional opposition between a philosophical and a political reading and submit texts such as Heidegger's to a double reading. Hence we can see, for example, sublimated anti-semitism in Heidegger's condemnation of 'wandering'.[7] It is this kind of double reading which will be applied here to Bourdieu's work.

The 1987–88 edition of the French *Who's Who* reveals that Pierre Bourdieu was born in 1930 at Denguin in the Lower Pyrenees. It lists his father's profession as 'functionary'. In keeping with his ideas about the necessary 'self-reflexivity' of the sociologist, Bourdieu does not hesitate to find a place in his theories for the circumstances of his birth and upbringing. He insists on numerous occasions that the intellectual or sociologist/scientist must become aware of the process by which he distances himself from the object of his study, noting that the 'theoretical' vision of a particular situation is quite different from the lived or 'practical' view. To engage in effective sociology it is necessary to understand the difference between the 'practical mode of existence of those who do not have the liberty to place the world at a distance'[8] and the experience of the scientist who sees the world from the carefully fabricated 'exteriority' of 'theory'. Bourdieu notes that as a 'mountain peasant' he had the opportunity to experience directly what it means to exist in practical proximity to a particular social world. Thus, when he returned to his native region to conduct an ethnological study,[9] he was in a particularly good position to become aware of the differences that divide 'practical' and 'theoretical' views of the world.[10] Not all of

Bourdieu's critics have been entirely convinced by these arguments, however, and two of them go so far as to conclude sardonically: 'the moral of the story is obvious; if you weren't a mountain peasant, preferably socially indigenous, you run every risk of becoming a bad sociologist'.[11]

More generally, the theme of difference, of feeling displaced, of being an outsider in the bourgeois setting of the Parisian intellectual world is a constant theme in Bourdieu's work and one he frequently invokes to explain his interest in analysing and 'objectifying' his own intellectual milieu and the educational institutions within which he works. As he remarks in an interview, he feels

> a stranger in the intellectual world . . . I don't feel at home. I feel I owe somebody an explanation—but who? I have no idea. I feel I owe somebody an explanation for what appears to me to be an unjustified privilege. This experience, I believe, can be recognised in many of those who are socially stigmatised.[12]

It must be noted, however, that Bourdieu left his native region when he was quite young to study at the prestigious Louis-le-Grand Lycée in Paris, going on to study at the Faculty of Letters in Paris at the École Normale Supérieure. He began his career as a high school teacher at Moulins in 1955, then moved on to become an assistant or tutor in the Arts faculty at Algiers from 1958 to 1960. He returned to Paris to work as an assistant in 1960 to 1961 and then went on to take up a lecturing position in Lille from 1961 to 1964. In 1964, he became a *directeur d'études* at the École Pratique des Hautes Études in Paris and finally in 1981 was appointed to the chair of Sociology at the Collège de France. Michel Foucault, incidentally, was a strong supporter of Bourdieu's candidacy. In Bourdieu's inaugural speech there are in fact quite a number of indirect allusions to Foucault's work and to the first few pages of Foucault's own inaugural speech in 1970.[13]

Many of these institutions, however, are quite mysterious to the Anglo-Saxon reader, and it might be useful, in the best tradition of Bourdieu's own interest in the sociology of institutions and intellectuals, to make some comments about them at this stage. First of all, the Lycée Louis-le-Grand. It is interesting to note that a large proportion of France's intelligentsia (writers, theorists, journalists, publishers, academics, politicians and so on) went to the same lycées and that those lycées are all in Paris. This does not mean, however, that France's intellectuals all come from Paris, as the case of Bourdieu illustrates. In fact about 50 per cent of the Parisian intelligentsia originally came from the provinces. The most prestigious lycées are, in order, Louis-le-Grand, Henri-IV, and Janson de Sailly. As Hamon and Rotman say in their highly readable and controversial book *Les Intellocrates*: 'outside Paris, no salvation. One can understand that the Breton, the Béarnais or the Picard admitted to one of these fetish institutions experiences a sensation comparable to that of an athlete selected for the Olympics'.[14] At Louis-le-Grand in the period immediately after the war, we find Pierre Bourdieu, Jacques Le-Goff, Jean-François Lyotard and Alain Touraine. At Henri IV we find Michel Foucault, Gilles Deleuze, René Girard and the historians Emmanuel Le Roy Ladurie, André Burguière and Pierre Vidal Naquet. Bourdieu is described in his school reports as 'a model of seriousness and method, but not very lively'. Jacques Derrida, also at Louis-le-Grand, is described as a 'solid and hardworking pupil'.[15] Many of these students then went on to the École Normale Supérieure in the Rue d'Ulm. Technically, one could describe this institution as a very prestigious teacher's training college, but it has in fact more status than the universities, and people who have been through the Rue d'Ulm together tend to form a mutual self-help group, much to the annoyance of those intellectuals unlucky enough *not* to have passed through this venerable institution.[16]

The institution now known as the École des Hautes Études en Sciences Sociales (EHESS), where Bourdieu is currently based, was originally established as the '6th section' of the École Pratique des Hautes Études in 1947 by the two 'Annales' historians, Fernand Braudel and Lucien Febvre. In 1968, the various centres and laboratories of the 6th section were finally housed by the efforts of Braudel under the same roof at the Maison des Sciences de l'Homme, a modern and well-equipped building on the Boulevard Raspail in Paris. A few years later in 1975, the '6th section' became the autonomous institution that exists today.[17] Looking through the list of seminars offered for any one year is a bit like consulting a who's who of French intellectual life. Robert Badinter, Bourdieu, Derrida, Luc Ferry, Maurice Godelier and Cornelius Castoriadis and, of course, members of the famous Annales school of historians are all listed as offering courses for the 1988–89 academic year. As François Furet, now nominated France's number one intellectual, jokes: 'I don't know what the Annales school is, but I meet it in the lift every day'.[18] And as Hamon and Rotman remark:

> the École concentrates within its walls a formidable intellectual *force de frappe* unique in France. To penetrate into this fortress of knowledge is not the absolute guarantee that you are acceding to

the Pantheon of the mind, but here, more than anywhere else you are getting close.[19]

If the historians at the École tend to form a closely knit group, the same does not apply to the sociologists. Bourdieu remarks of that other famous sociologist at the École, Alain Touraine: 'Between Touraine and me, there is an irreconcilable division. This opposition is a scientific one. People who have an absolutely exclusive approach to the discipline cannot coexist in sociology. If I'm right what he is doing is not sociology. It's him or me'.[20] The rivalry between Bourdieu and Touraine at the school is well known and surfaced on the occasion of Bourdieu's election to the Collège de France in 1981, when Bourdieu was elected rather than Touraine. Bourdieu explains to Hamon and Rotman that if he was not interested in the social advantages of holding a position at the Collège de France, he considered a certain 'intellectual capital' to be at stake. 'Personally, I couldn't care less', he declares, 'but socially I have to care. It is one of the only places which is prestigious without being academic'.[21]

The Collège de France is indeed France's most prestigious intellectual institution. There are only 52 chairs and professors are only obliged to teach two hours a week for thirteen weeks of the year. These lectures are open to the general public and can become high-society events. Roland Barthes, Foucault and Lévi-Strauss all taught there. A journalist describes rather well the atmosphere at the courses of one of these mandarins, Michel Foucault:

> As for a gala performance, there was a crush in front of the doors some two hours in advance. Inside, emissaries reserved places and it was a fight to the death to find a perch on the edge of a quarter of a folding seat. Women from the most exclusive neighbourhoods of Paris came decked out in their best designer clothes.[22]

Bourdieu's witty and entertaining courses are a similar event.

In addition to conducting his courses at the Collège and the École, Bourdieu continues to add to his formidable list of publications. His first book was published in 1958, his most recent in April 1989. A complete bibliography of his works and translations of his work, compiled by Yvette Delsault and published by the Centre de Sociologie Européenne, was published in December 1986 and an updated edition was under preparation in 1989.

Bourdieu's first book was an ethnographical and sociological study of Algeria published in 1958. Over the next few years he published several articles on Algeria and in 1962 became interested in the relations between the sexes in peasant communities. Then in 1964, in collaboration with Jean-Claude Passeron, he published his influential *Les Héretiers*, translated into English with a new epilogue in 1979. This book examines in a highly critical manner how knowledge is transmitted in the French education system. In 1965, this time in collaboration with three other authors, Bourdieu published a book on photography titled *Un art moyen: Essai sur les emplois sociaux de la photographie*. A revised edition was published in 1970. In 1966, Bourdieu collaborated again with two other writers to produce another book, *L'Amour de l'art: Les musées de l'art européens et leur public*. This was to be a precursor of Bourdieu's later vast and influential tome *La Distinction*, published in 1979. At the same time Bourdieu continued to publish articles on the transmission of culture in peasant societies as well as in the university. During the 1970s, like many other French writers, he became increasingly interested in the questions of power, cultural modes of domination and 'bodies'. In 1980 he published no less than three books: *Le Sens pratique, Questions de sociologie* and *Travaux et projets*. His work started to diversify considerably at this point, taking in topics such as Afghanistan, terrorism, death, Montesquieu, Sartre, regionalism, intellectuals, sociological studies of French bishops and the sociology of sport.

In 1982, Bourdieu's inaugural speech at the Collège de France was published, as well as a book titled *Ce que parler veut dire: L'économie de l'échange linguistique*. In 1984, Bourdieu published an excellent analysis of the workings of the academic world in France, *Homo Academicus*, which appeared in English translation in 1988. In 1985 he wrote about opinion polls, the Kanaks in New Caledonia, cultural history, Belgian literature, religion and power, the cultural practice of reading, and ethnology. In 1988 he published *L'Ontologie politique de Martin Heidegger*, a revised edition of a methodological essay he had originally published in 1975. He also wrote about Marcel Proust, for whose practice of writing he feels a close affinity.[23] In May 1989 he published *La Noblesse d'état: Les Grandes Écoles et esprit de corps* which deals with the way the *grandes écoles* function in forming elites in French society. Bourdieu has also edited the journal *Actes de la recherche en science sociales* since 1975. He frequently publishes short articles in this journal.

For all the immense variety of Bourdieu's interests and his extraordinarily impressive output, there are a number of themes which recur in his work. One is the epistemological status of sociology. On opening Bourdieu's most recent book, *La Noblesse d'état*, a reader familiar with his work is not surprised to see that the first paragraph

contains an apology for the science of sociology. Indeed, in almost
every book and article written after about 1965 he manages to make
some statement about the excellence of sociology and its scientific
virtues, particularly in relation to certain other less empirically based
disciplines such as philosophy. For Bourdieu 'sociology is an esoteric
science—the initiation is very slow and requires a veritable conver-
sion of a whole world vision'.[24] Sociology is a way of interpreting the
world, a means of gaining access to the truth about the world. If this
type of activity is generally considered to be the province of philosophy, Bourdieu would argue that sociology offers a far truer vision of
the world than does 'philosophy', especially given the latter's tendency to indulge in grandiose 'prophetic' and 'metaphysical' postur-
ing. Indeed, Bourdieu's scorn for philosophy is scathing and final, to
the point that after a particularly impassioned attack on prophetic
philosophers who ignore the empirical world in the style of
Heidegger, a shocked interviewer interrupts, 'You're exaggerating
there! I can't let you get away with saying that!'.[25] Certain questions
traditionally regarded as philosophical, according to Bourdieu, could
in fact be far more usefully reformulated in the 'scientific' language
of sociology.[26] And for the benefit of those who would question the
equation of science and sociology, he observes that in sociology one
finds 'coherent systems of hypotheses, concepts, methods of verifi-
cation, everything that is usually associated with the idea of science.
So why not say that sociology is a science if it is one? . . . One of the
ways of getting rid of annoying truths is to say they are not
scientific'.[27]

But for all this, 'science' is never neutral in Bourdieu's view; there
are always interests at stake, whether those of truth or power. Thus
the sociologist only produces the 'truth' because he has an interest or
investment in truth: 'This interest might be the desire to be first to
make a discovery and to appropriate to oneself all the associated
rights, or it might be moral indignation or the revolt against certain
forms of domination in the rest of the field'.[28] He also notes that a
number of sociologists perform the function of 'social engineers',
providing 'formulas for the directors of private enterprise and
bureaucracy'. He is highly critical of this state of affairs, remarking
that to 'ask sociology to be useful for something is always a way of
asking it to serve power'.[29] This declaration could easily be
generalised to all knowledge and could readily be applied to criticise
current technocratic policies in the area of education.

What is most interesting, perhaps, about these statements concerning sociology, truth and science which recur so frequently in
Bourdieu's work is the contradictory nature of the assumptions that

underlie them. First of all, Bourdieu argues that sociology is a science and, as he suggests in one of the above statements, to say that something is scientific is to guarantee its truth, its distinction from 'ideology'. But Bourdieu is fully aware of discussions concerning the problematic nature of the science/ideology distinction and hastens to add that science and the search for truth are never neutral. Yet somehow his own science of sociology escapes from the problems intrinsic to other approaches. In fact, the correct practice of sociology would eventually lead to the exposure of the real if somewhat bleak truth about our social world. As he remarks: 'Sometimes I wonder whether the completely transparent and disenchanted social universe that would be produced by a fully developed social science would not be unlivable'.[30] But he still thinks a kind of lucid despair is better than the comfort of illusion. Bourdieu's *La Distinction* and *Homo Academicus* are particularly good examples of his approach. In both these works all artistic, intellectual and educational enterprise become primarily the means of reinforcing social distinction and positions within institutional hierarchies. All social interaction is, in the end, reduced to relations between dominators and dominated. To aspire to be educated is ultimately no more than to aspire to a more elevated position in the social hierarchy. Any resistance to the status quo becomes no more than the consequence of social misplacement, the inability, for whatever reason, to find one's 'natural' and socially preordained niche in the social body. Hence a young unemployed person with a devalued Arts degree, having been given certain expectations by society which are no longer met, tends to react by resisting the status quo.[31] Every aesthetic judgment or judgment of taste becomes a strategy of social distinction. Even 'falling in love' can be seen as an expression of taste (the taste for someone with similar tastes).[32] Or as Luc Ferry and Alain Renaut suggest:

> If the bourgeois serves sausages for dinner, it is through snobbism, trying to show that he's not so different from the working class: thus he demonstrates a typically bourgeois attitude, and if he prefers to serve smoked salmon, well there is no longer any doubt about the diagnosis (My God, it's obvious!). How is it that under these conditions, Bourdieu didn't die of hunger long ago?[33]

On a more serious note, the tone of Bourdieu's work, particularly in *La Distinction*, is highly critical. No one escapes, peasant, worker or bourgeois, yet any attempt at resistance and criticism can equally well be encompassed within this inexorable system. Nonetheless, this is far from being Bourdieu's conscious intention. As he says, 'an unknown law is a nature or destiny ... A known law appears as the

PIERRE BOURDIEU

possibility of freedom'.[34] If a social agent is aware of the laws governing his situation or behaviour, he may choose to either accept or reject those laws instead of acting ignorantly under blind compulsion. The aim is to provide people with the possibility of assuming their lot 'without guilt or suffering'.[35] But unfortunately the logic of Bourdieu's schema means that the rejection of any set of laws is merely the result of a second set of laws ultimately only leading to the adoption of yet another system of rules. At no point does the system break down into uncertainty or fade into nothingness or chaos. All can be quite safely explained within its parameters.[36]

But for all these difficulties, touched on only briefly here, there are a great number of interesting and useful questions raised by Bourdieu's work. I should like to conclude by drawing attention to what is perhaps its most striking and valuable aspect, namely Bourdieu's ability to apply 'very abstract schemas to very concrete things', and his ability to detect the mundane everyday world of concrete objects and practices in the most 'noble' and 'elevated' systems of thought such as that proposed by Heidegger, for example. 'Reading the statistics of how many people wear pyjamas while thinking about Kant is not that obvious', he remarks. 'The whole educational process tends to prevent one from thinking about Kant in relation to pyjamas or about pyjamas while reading Marx.'[37] This type of thought emerges for example in a passage from *Distinction* about the statistics of the consumption of bedroom slippers in France:

> Small industrial and commercial employers, the incarnation of the 'grocer' traditionally execrated by artists, are the category who most often (60 percent) say they change into their slippers every day before dinner, whereas the professions and the senior executives are most inclined to reject this petit-bourgeois symbol (35 percent say they never do it). The particularly high consumption of slippers by working-class women (both urban and rural) no doubt reflects the relation to the body and self-presentation entailed by confinement to the home and to domestic life. (The wives of craftsmen, shopkeepers and manual workers are those who most often say that their choice of clothes is mainly guided by a concern to please their husbands.)[38]

One can clearly see in this passage how Bourdieu applies Kant (aesthetics) and Marx (notions of class) to the apparently mundane practice of wearing slippers. In *L'Ontologie politique de Martin Heidegger* he applies the same process in reverse and shows how the 'abstract' categories of Heidegger's thought are a transposition of certain very concrete and less than noble social and political ideas. It is this constant interplay between the humdrum monotony of everyday social interaction and the most abstract offerings of 'high culture' that traverses all of Bourdieu's work that makes it one of the most fascinating and enlightening reflections on the relation between the social world and its cultural institutions to emerge in recent years.

NOTES

This chapter was written with the assistance of a Postdoctoral Research Fellowship at the University of Melbourne. The author wishes to thank in particular the School of Social Theory and the Department of History and Philosophy of Science.

1 For the reader unfamiliar with Bourdieu's work, his *La Distinction: Critique sociale du jugement* Paris: Minuit, 1979 (translated 1984) provides perhaps the best starting point. For an excellent overview of Bourdieu's works and comments on its reception in English see Loïc J. D. Wacquant 'Toward a reflexive sociology: A workshop with Pierre Bourdieu' *Sociological Theory* 7, 1989, pp. 26–63. For two useful and recent interviews see Bourdieu 'For a socio-analysis of intellectuals *Berkeley Journal of Sociology* 34, 1989, pp. 1–29 and 'Social space and symbolic power' *Sociological Theory* 7, Spring, 1989, pp. 18–26).

2 See *Lire* April 1981 and *L'Événement du jeudi* February 1989. An interesting article by Bourdieu which questions the validity of such intellectual 'hit parades' is included as an appendix to *Homo Academicus* (Paris: Minuit, 1984): 'Le hit-parade des intellectuels français ou qui sera juge de la legitimité des juges?'.

3 For a good discussion of 'theory' and 'the kind of conceptual gobbledygook' that passes by that name, see Bourdieu 'From the Sociology of Academics to the Sociology of the Sociological Eye' *Sociological Theory* 7, 1, 1989, interview with Loïc J. D. Wacquant, section titled 'The Refusal of "Theoretical Theory" '.

4 In his prefaces to the English translations of *La Distinction* and *Homo Academicus* (1988), Bourdieu comments on the importance of understanding the French context of his writings and how his ideas might be adapted by a process of analogy and cultural translation to the English-speaking context. He notes that there is always a danger that the 'exotic' French setting might reduce the critical force of his ideas for the foreign reader who, lacking the necessary information, will not make the appropriate cultural translation. To use a very simple example, in the Australian setting beer is drunk by roughly the same social sort of person who drinks cheap wine in France. In addition, the sort of academic power games that Bourdieu describes in *Homo Academicus* are by no means restricted to the French academic world.

5 On the notion of ideas as historical and social practices, see in particular Paul Veyne *Comment on écrit l'histoire suivi de Foucault revolutionne l'histoire* Paris: Seuil, 1978 and the excellent encyclopedia/dictionary edited by Jacques Le Goff et al. *La Nouvelle Histoire* Paris: Retz-CEPL, Les

encyclopédies du savoir moderne, 1978 (particularly the entries by Philippe Ariès). See also Michel Foucault 'Débat avec Michel Foucault: table ronde du 20 mai 1978' in Michelle Perrot (ed.) *L'Impossible Prison: recherches sur le système pénitentiaire au XIXe siècle* Paris: Seuil, 1980, pp. 29–56.

6 P. Bourdieu *L'Ontologie politique de Martin Heidegger* Paris: Minuit, p. 10

7 ibid. p. 7

8 P. Bourdieu *Le Sens pratique* Paris: Minuit, 1980, p. 30

9 See P. Bourdieu 'Les Relations entre les sexes dans la société paysanne' *Les Temps modernes* 195, August 1962, pp. 307–31; 'Célibat et condition paysanne' *Études rurales* 5–6, April 1962, pp. 32–136.

10 *Le Sens pratique* p. 30. Bourdieu develops his arguments on 'objectifying objectification' at length in this work. See also the excellent collection of interviews contained in *Choses Dites* Paris: Minuit, 1987, pp. 32–33, 75–76, 108–9, 112–16; *Homo Academicus* ch. 1, pp. 11–52; 'From the Sociology of Academics'; and the preface to the English translation of *Homo Academicus* (1988).

11 Luc Ferry and Alain Renaut *La Pensée 68: Essais sur l'anti-humanisme contemporain* Paris: Gallimard, 1988, p. 257. This entertaining but perhaps somewhat hastily researched work caused quite a stir when it hit the bookshops.

12 P. Bourdieu *Questions de sociologie* Paris: Minuit, 1980, p. 76

13 See P. Bourdieu *Leçon sur la leçon* Paris: Minuit, 1982, p. 7; Michel Foucault *L'Ordre du discours* Paris: Gallimard, pp. 7–10.

14 H. Hamon and P. Rotman *Les Intellocrates: Expédition en haute intelligentsia*: Paris: Ramsay, 1981, 2nd edn, Éditions Complexe, 1985. Much of the following information on French educational institutions is drawn from this book.

15 ibid. p. 218. Bourdieu observes that such notions as being gifted, talented and possessing style and taste are mere euphemisms serving to preserve social inequalities. Less privileged students with limited cultural capital are obliged to work hard to acquire what seems to come 'naturally' to the privileged few and are branded as 'swots' for their efforts ('The school as a conservative force', 1974, pp. 38–40).

16 For valuable remarks on this 'great lay seminary' which is the ENS, see the preface to the English edition of *Homo Academicus*. For further comments on the way the ENS has functioned and continues to function as an institution which trains the political, industrial and intellectual elites in French society see Bourdieu's most recent study, *La Noblesse d'État: Grandes Écoles et esprit de corps* Paris: Minuit, 1989, esp. pp. 64–81. Bourdieu notes that the prestige and power has in recent decades shifted from the ENS to the École Nationale d'Administration (ENA). See also 'Le Pouvoir n'est plus Rue-d'Ulm', interview with Didier Eribon *Le Nouvel Observateur* 9 March, 1989, pp. 80–82 and ibid. pp. 32–33.

17 For remarks on the history of the EHESS and on the Annales school of historians who both founded this institution and ensured its prestige see Hamon and Rotman *Les Intellocrates* pp. 40–49; Guy Bourdé and Hervé Martin *Les Écoles historiques* Paris: Seuil, 1983, pp. 204–7; Traian Stoianovich *French Historical Method: The Annales Paradigm* Ithaca: Cornell University Press, 1976; François Dosse *L'Histoire en miettes: Des*

'*Annales*' *à la* '*nouvelle histoire*' Paris: La Découverte, 1987, pp. 119–27; Hervé Coutau-Begarie *Le Phénomène 'Nouvelle Histoire': Stratégie et idéologie des nouveaux historiens* Paris: Économica, 1983, pp. 260–68.

18 Hamon and Rotman *Les Intellocrates* p. 45
19 ibid. p. 40
20 ibid pp. 45–46
21 ibid p. 51
22 Gerard Lefort 'Au Collège de France: Un judoka de l'intellect' *Libération* 26 June 1984, p. 6
23 *Choses Dites* p. 66
24 ibid p. 68
25 P. Bourdieu 'Heidegger par Pierre Bourdieu: le krach de la philosophie', interview with Robert Maggiori *Libération* 10 March, 1988, p. 6. Or as another interviewer remarks more mildly, 'Like many sociologists, you are not particularly indulgent towards philosophers' *(Choses Dites* p. 53). For a selection of comments on the relative merits of sociology and philosophy see also pp. 13–46, 53–55 and *L'Ontologie politique* pp. 7–14.
26 *Questions de sociologie* p. 50
27 ibid. p. 21
28 ibid. p. 23
29 ibid. pp. 27–28
30 *Questions de Sociologie* p. 33. For another remark in the same vein see *Choses Dites* pp. 25–26: '[The sociologist] takes the despair of the absolutist humanist to its limits in displaying necessity in contingency, in revealing the system of social conditions which has made a particular way of being or doing possible, thus necessitated without being necessary. The sociologist does nothing but reveal and bring out into the light of day the wretchedness of man without God, of man without a preordained destiny, and he is made responsible for that wretchedness like all prophets of doom. One may well slay the messenger, but what he has announced will remain and be heard'.
31 Cf. *La Distinction* pp. 159–69 and *Questions de sociologie* p. 76.
32 *La Distinction* pp. 267–71; *Choses Dites* p. 88
33 Ferry and Renaut *La Pensée* 68 p. 279
34 *Questions de sociologie* p. 45; cf. *Choses Dites* pp. 25–26.
35 *Questions de sociologie* p. 42
36 Baudrillard applies a similar criticism to Foucault's theories of power in *Oublier Foucault* Paris: Galilée, 1977, pp. 54–55. See also Ferry and Renaut *La Pensée* 68 pp. 239–79.
37 *Questions de sociologie* p. 40
38 *Distinction* p. 187; *La Distinction* p. 208

PART IV
A Symposium

As more space in bookshops is given over for the latest translations of French theory, and as more students are enrolling for courses in post-structuralist thought, it seems important to seize the moment and evaluate what this trend might have to offer. The overall involvement of contributors in recent French thought and the concerns they share about its reception prompted the idea of a symposium which would examine more generally the uses of French theory in an Anglo context. This provided the contributors with the opportunity to speak for French theory in general, rather than the case of a specific author.

Kevin Hart considers the differing intellectual contexts of French theory in France and the United States and argues for an active use of deconstructive theory. For Brenda Ludeman, the phenomenon of theory itself is something which is subject to question by French thought. David Odell also questions the 'usefulness' of theory and considers carefully how the kind of thinking in French theory is different from the Anglo tradition of thought. For Peter Cotton, this question is placed in the context of a phenomenological tradition where thinking has more at stake than the accumulation of knowledge. Chris McAuliffe considers the tactical usefulness of French theory within a specific cultural setting—he opposes this to the evaluation of French theory as 'fashion'. While Julian Pefanis also grants importance to the cultural uses of French theory, he sees the possibilities of fiction as more appropriate to its use than those of philosophy. Finally, Clare O'Farrell outlines how French theory might be used to create a kind of 'club' in Anglo societies, but points out as well how it can be useful in particular arguments such as that currently occurring about the status of universities.

Where the contributors seem to differ is in the generality of the project within which French theory might be placed: whether it concerns the 'source of Being' or a specific political agenda. In general, however, the several points of view in the symposium serve to outline the edge at which French theory meets the local form of Anglo thought.

10 The uses of recent French theory

KEVIN HART

I thought I'd start by just giving us a moment to remind ourselves what deconstruction is, at least as I understand it. It seems to me that deconstruction, and I mean by that mainly Derridean deconstruction, has three related moments. The first is a recognition that western thought is covertly organised into a powerful system of structured oppositions. This system is not simply a construct of idealism; it's not simply synchronic; it's also a material, historical phenomenon. It has a particular history, and it influences the courses of history. The second moment of deconstruction is a critique of that system, both its grounding concepts and its genealogy. It's a critique that first determines then works from a point which is 'other' than the spaces generated by the western imagination. And it's the realm of the 'other', that point neither inside nor outside the system, which Derrida famously calls *différance*, or *arche-écriture*, or *supplément*. The third point is the transformation of that system, and this involves, as Derrida says, a 'thinking otherwise' of its central questions. It is a style of thinking which meshes with specific material practices while also redistributing their premises. And I suppose it's with that third moment in particular, the moment of transformation, that we begin to see the practical uses of deconstruction. I would stress, though, that these three moments are not discrete phases; each implies the other, and there is no uninterrupted line between 'theory' and 'practice'. I think it would be naive to argue that philosophical discourses are isolated from politics and the everyday, as one sometimes finds argued with respect to Derrida and French theory. I suppose the most complicated, erudite, Alexandrian theory that any philosopher has ever proposed is Hegel's system; but it doesn't take much to see what Marx has done with Hegelianism, and everything one sees in the twentieth century is touched in one way or another by certain motifs, certain themes, of Hegel. They have been reworked in the dominant political codes of Russia, China and Eastern Europe. Their influence is enormous. Deconstruction tells us, in fact, that notions which are often taken to be non-philosophical, entirely quotidian—value, property, work, economics, the family, the university, or whatever—are riven with philosophical concepts. Institutions such as the family and the university certainly have a material history, but that history is tightly interwoven with the history of metaphysics. The two are inseparable. So apparently non-philosophical problems, issues which aren't usually discussed in philosophy seminars, (questions of technology, nuclear war, political interventions in the academy ...) arise from within the history of philosophy as well as within material history. I think this is something that needs to be emphasised because, as I understand it, deconstruction is not merely the study of formal undecidability, as is sometimes promoted. Decisions are made every day of the week, as everyone knows, and deconstruction involves the study of specific historical decisions, the reductions they make and the effects they have. Quite clearly, many of these decisions are overtly political, and even those which are not may have interesting political consequences.

Well, how are we to put deconstruction to work in practical situations? In answering this question, we have to keep a couple of things in mind. First, we must recognise that practical problems are part of a highly structured and powerful economy of concepts. What Derrida offers us, I think, is a vocabulary which enables us to trace the laws of that economy, and a series of strategies which allow us to turn that economy against itself. In other words, no decision is simply an individual's, even though it may seem so at any given time. The individual is empowered by an institution which has a particular history that encourages a range of decisions. Second, this economy must be displaced and transformed by means of its most intimate concepts. We transform a given state of affairs only when we begin to think its grounding questions otherwise. There is no way out of it: we must do the hard work and think through the genealogy of western thought, noting *both* the decisions that have been made *and* the elements which have been significantly repressed, overlooked or reduced. Only then can we confidently reinscribe those forgotten elements into our discussions, debates and actions. One of the things I admire in Derrida is that he does not prescribe how we are to do that: he is very open to a range of futures for deconstruction. He is more open to chance, difference, and variety than many of his disciples. When you think about it, deconstruction has often been received as a narrow, dogmatic message from Paris, as though Derrida were a latter-day *philosophe*. Deconstruction is frequently identified with anti-theological motifs, whereas if you read his work closely, you can hear something quite different. To be sure, Derrida has some stringent criticisms of metaphysical theology, eschatology and messianic movements, but he also offers a critique of secular modernity, atheism and the 'death of God' group. When set to work in religious contexts, deconstruction does not ask us to become atheists or agnostics, but it does invite us to think God otherwise. The fact that Jacques Derrida does not happen to be interested in pursuing this line of enquiry does not make it unavailable to us. If anything, it makes it more challenging, more inviting.

This notion of 'thinking otherwise' involves at least two things. First of all, there's a very practical intervention in definite codeable situations, which can be party politics, gender politics, institutional conflicts, or whatever. (It's important to remember that, as a mode of analysis, deconstruction has no assertive power whatsoever. It is a mode of destructuring, of deconstituting. There is a moment in which the other is affirmed; but you cannot posit anything from a deconstructive point of view. That's one reason why many deconstructionists are interested in figures of strength in history, whether material history or the history of metaphysics, art, religion ... Those who can only analyse, important though that may be, are drawn to those who claim strength.) At the same time as this intervention, deconstruction requires us to put pressure on the vocabulary and the concepts of the situation in which we are engaged. So one is disrupting the official codes, finding gaps, differences, heterogeneities—in short, what has remained unthought or repressed.

So deconstruction is, among other things, a critique of totality. And this is worth pondering for a moment; for it is by no means self-evident that this is always and everywhere a good thing. Fredric Jameson makes the point very eloquently in *The Political Unconscious* that critiques of totalisation carry different weights in different contexts. It is one thing to broach such a critique in France, where centralism is regarded as politically dubious value; quite another in America where the Left suffers precisely because of its fragmentation, its inability to cohere into a unified front. What may have been an object of deconstruction in Paris circa 1968 is not necessarily what needs to be passed under review in Melbourne circa 1988. It is important to stress that deconstruction is not a formula, that it carries no specific political agenda or political rhetoric. Or rather, that when it becomes a formula or hardens into political doctrines, it no longer has life and critical force.

I've been talking about the uses of deconstruction, but in conclusion I'd like to say something about how it may be abused. Now in putting the matter that way I open myself to a range of objections. How can deconstruction, which is always a critique of the proper, be said to have proper and improper uses? That's a question we might like to discuss later on. We could talk, for instance, of the 'Paul de Man' affair, that matrix of issues concerning whether deconstruction is covertly in league with fascism or sets itself to dismantle that politics. Or we could talk about whether deconstruction is a formalism, a set of ways of rereading the canon but not questioning the uses to which the canon is put. For now I'd just like to pick out two things.

The first is a kind of political use of deconstruction that one finds associated with Derrida. To be sure, Derrida has been very keen to put deconstruction to work in the service of left-wing aims. You can see this in his work for GREPH in trying to save and extend the teaching of philosophy in secondary schools, his interrogation of the apartheid system in South Africa, and his contribution to the protests about nuclear weapons. Quite opposed to this politically engaged style of critique is what I would like to call 'angelic' deconstruction, a formalist mode of literary criticism (greatly indebted to the new criticism) which is only concerned with examining a text and showing that, in the end, we cannot decide what it really means. Thus in American literary criticism of a deconstructionist stamp we see a powerful vocabulary of *différance*, *supplément*, and *dissemination* relapse into an empty formalism, a style of criticism that circles around the aesthetic as a prized category, and remains uninterested in questions of ideology. Barbara Johnson makes the point with her customary lucidity when contrasting two of her books. In the first collection of essays, *The Critical Difference*, the author seems to say 'Here is a text; let me read it'; while in the second collection, *A World of Difference*, she adds the question, 'Why am I reading *this* text?'

That kind of move, taking formal and social questions in tandem, is very attractive to me. But here's a caveat. One has to be very careful, very vigilant, in using the vocabulary of deconstruction, especially Derrida's vocabulary, which was so prominent after 1968. It sounds so subversive, muscular and ideologically sound; but taken by itself (if that were possible), deconstruction is not necessarily of the Left. Using a vocabulary partly influenced by marxism does not automatically make you politically respectable, any more than using words like 'justice', 'hope' and 'forgiveness' makes you a Christian. As soon as you remove deconstruction from its originary signifying system and place it in another context, it changes. It is one of the principal axioms that such change is bound to occur. All texts, including *Of Grammatology*, *Margins of Philosophy*, *Glas*, and the rest, are subject to being inscribed in unforeseen, chance contexts; their messages can be deflected from their original destinations. Deconstruction in Paris in 1968 is one thing. But it must be studied without pathos, without nostalgia, if we are to learn anything from it. If you agree with Derrida's arguments about interpretation, the nature of communication, and the history of philosophy, then you have to agree that deconstruction must change from time to time and from place to place. What you make of deconstruction will depend in part on where you find it at work and where you propose to put it to work. If you are a writer, how does deconstruction help you to read and write? (And not just those writers Derrida reads, but those *you* read.) And if you are a painter, how does deconstruction help you to see and paint? There are the kind of questions that might keep French theory in play in Melbourne, and expose it to the risks of change. They are questions we have to ask ourselves and of each other, and we can begin that now.

BRENDA LUDEMAN

Aphemia means loss of articulation; one may still have access to words yet one is unable to signify. In *The Slut of The Normandy Coast* Marguerite Duras describes her inability to complete a piece of writing: 'I had been emptied out, I had become the opposite of a writer'. To be aphemic is to give up that position which a symbolic function demands, to be the opposite of one who is able to signify. The aphemic 'writer' suppresses the codes of syntax and resists the symbolic mode (albeit without recourse to (in)sanity) in order that another discourse might be spoken. Those who would capitalise the word Theory deny that which is speculative and propositional in theoretical analysis. Nevertheless a project such as that of Julia Kristeva requires a form of reading which allows for the 'anaphoric', the 'elsewhere' of meaning.

DAVID ODELL

I begin by quoting two writers, neither of whom is French. One is William Blake who says: 'I must create my own system or be enslaved by another man's'. And the other, Ralph Waldo Emerson who says in the essay 'Self Reliance' something like: 'In reading the works of others we encounter our own unthought thoughts which gaze back at us with an alienated majesty'. Reading Emerson, somewhat against the grain, I would want to stress not only 'self reliance', the point that Blake makes with justifiable urgency, but also the way that in all our reading, and in a broader sense all our textual engagements, we always find ourselves already complicit, perhaps in surprising and 'alienating' ways, with other men's (and I retain Blake's masculine emphasis advisedly) systems.

I believe that only by doing battle against theory (and not only in its received forms) do we have a chance to begin forging our own theoretical sphere.

But why should we need or want to do that?

Not to pay the others back, to show them, or to be recognised at last by them, but to make this place possible as a dwelling place for thinking. Or to express this differently: because we are continually discovering that we are already part of a thinking. Someone or some system seems to have supplied all our words and concepts, and so at the limits of our world, which at each moment are right next to us, there is a murmur going on of other negotiations from which we are not only excluded by non-presence but which bear no relation to the possibilities of our spaces. There is an oppressive quality to this which theoretical struggle needs to overturn.

Why use the word 'theory'?

In so far as it has implications of system, of an attempt to comprehensively explain and control on the basis of a schematism which complacently substitutes abstract counters for realities, the word itself needs to be reinterpreted. I think that these implications, which arise out of a certain popular cultural understanding of 'science' which is heavily freighted with ideology, are out of place in the sense in which we ought to envisage theory. There is a kind of discourse which resembles theory, in that scientific sense, in seeming to have a surface of abstraction but which is rather an elaboration of the position from which the shortcomings of theory become evident. This is what is called theory, but the name must always remain open to contestation. It serves best to distinguish it from philosophy. Theory is more portable, more piecemeal, more idiosyncratic, more bricolable, than philosophy. It wears its contradictions more openly. The word, as a collective noun, just means 'views'. Theory in France is certainly spilt philosophy, but this is no bad thing; it is perhaps the only form in which thinking can continue: philosophy psychoanalysed but not necessarily cured.

Why would one want to preserve thinking?

Perhaps out of nostalgia for adolescence when one still thought thinking mattered. Perhaps because of an ineradicable reflex that still calls upon thinking to resolve the mess we find ourselves in, a mess itself made up of shards of thought, of the fragmentary words of philosophers around which massive blind practices and cultures seem to elaborate themselves. Perhaps only because thinking seems to be able rigorously to destroy the illusion of freedom that thinking engenders. If there is a sort of nostalgia associated with the idea of thinking as something capable of taking us to the depths, then this is the aura of philosophy. But if philosophy works its wonderful spells because of a supposed universality in language, which makes it capable of approaching or housing the really big things, and if it is just this universality which we can no longer accept, if our language is local through and through, how can we continue to respond to the imperative of something like depth? We want a thinking that knows this question.

Is there a compelling reason why a form of thinking needs to be the response? Are there not other modes (transplanted here) which challenge the same ground, other ways of exploring the possibilities which are perhaps less cerebral, less wordy, more intuitive? Is it a matter of life and death?

All of these are doomed to futility unless we find a way to the problems which are presupposed in the way that such modes understand themselves. Critical theorising which draws on the depth of thinking, where what makes things possible as the things they might become, encounters itself, is the only way to elaborate our ground, that is, it traces the many folds of the dis-pens-ation which is the horizon of our individual and collective constitutions. It is likely that this dispensation is more empty, that is, lighter, than we suspect. This is not to say that artistic practices necessarily stand or fall according as their co-present explanatory or critical discourses stand or fall in the theoretical arena—although this often seems to be the case, especially as artists sensing the heat and dust give more weight to a discursive component in their works. Retrospectively art works are often seen to have anticipated theoretical developments, but this also means that these works go on being born in modes of thinking which they do not determine. The interrelations here are very complex since conscious awareness of the permeability of the barriers that defined traditional aesthetics (and they have always been permeable) now seems to be mandatory. But I want to stress that criticism as it exists at the moment is not the sort of theoretical thinking that

151

is called for; such thinking, long and painful in its gestation, will inhabit the landscape more than the pages of our reviews without being any the less a matter of words.

What sorts of projects would seem to attend to the possibility of a local thinking?

Perhaps one of the things that is called for is the careful examination of the empiricist pragmatist heritage of our British forebears. French thought represents not so much an alternative we might adopt to save us from what seems deadening in that heritage, an unthinking flight from a subjection to a regime of the hard-nosed fact as transplanted by the first fleet, as a point of reference which we can, to some extent, adopt outside that system in order to begin to see where its torsions and doublings are located. Having said that I should add that I don't think we can treat any sort of serious thinking instrumentally, in the way people these days talk about technologies, in the plural, as if there were a sort of supermarket.

While the major negotiation for theory is between philosophy and the sort of polymorphous criticism that rallies around the slogan of the 'death of theory', the one that concerns us particularly is that between various streams of thought which we are always aware of and which affect us materially, but which remain marked by their historical and national origins. So-called French theory for many of us, and I certainly speak for myself here, is mediated through its North American reception. But for Americans it brings something back to them which has been lost and suffered a sea-change; and I am thinking not only of the filiations of the eighteenth-century revolutions, but of Poe as inspiration for the symbolists and Nietzsche's affinity for Emerson. Pragmatism, the American metaphysic, seems pretty thin stuff after Hegel but is capable of powering some complex speculative moments. In this sense it differs profoundly from empiricism, which together with certain of its romantic variants is our central heritage. Perhaps we have our own incipient pragmatism, but mostly it seems that our Australian version of pragmatism is cynicism. French theory from its apprenticeship in Kantian and Hegelian philosophy thinks transcendentally and dialectically, that is, it tries to go to the conditions of possibility of its matters and it tries to work with and within contradictions. Both of these are hard for us to do from within the moral bastions of colonial empiricism. I think in particular that finding ways of sustaining oneself in and feeding on contradictions, but in a rigorous way at the same time, would be immensely valuable. Perhaps 'multiculturalism' is an approach to this from within officially sponsored ideology but which in some ways makes the task all the harder:

Does theory promise anything? Is there any way in which we can be sure we are on the right track, or are the sterner delights of theory to do with getting even more lost?
Perhaps theory is a form of death, in that it is the elaboration of moments when life ceases to be expansive, ceases to be able to surrender itself wholeheartedly to the moment. Thinking: the long way around, the operation of *ressentiment*, the carefully planned and inexorable revenge of the one who is denied the substance and possesses the abstraction. But in another sense there may be nothing more lively than such a death. The assurance of things being on the right track seems to me neither desirable nor possible, in that order; rather I would always seek a way back to tracklessness. But this is skirting around a kind of language which in the absence of a way of being extended dialectically slides into paradox.

Thinking is what is lost when the meaning generated by a complex utterance is grounded in empiricist pragmatist terms. The more aesthetically sensitive, the better the taste, the more thorough the loss. The latter is all we are genuinely given and where we must begin to think is in the sense of that loss, the loss which occurs when we begin to attempt to explain things to ourselves in the empiricist pragmatical language which comes so naturally to us.

PETER COTTON

> Unless human being first becomes established, before all else, in the space proper to its manner of temporal perduring (*wesen*) and there takes up its dwelling, it will not be capable of anything essential within the destining of Being now holding sway.
>
> Martin Heidegger (1962)

I am not at all clear about the general 'usefulness' of the work of recent French theorists and I think that there is a deeply realised ambivalence characterising their significance in our local context. To begin with, we need to pause and not pass too quickly over a notion like 'usefulness', which itself seems to be ambiguous. It could be that in our current world, the taken-for-granted sense of what constitutes usefulness no longer holds us exclusively within its sway. As such, it becomes open to question because it no longer goes without saying; perhaps because the very nature of the relationship between knowledge and action has become an issue for 'thinking' in a more radical manner than could hitherto be thematised. To clarify further this state of affairs, and to establish a context within which I can say something about recent French theory, I would like to draw on the understanding of our present world developed in recent phenomenological work . . .

Merleau-Ponty once said that Husserl's phenomenology began as a project to gain intellectual possession of the world and ended up revealing the limits of rationality and the inexorable 'shadow' of things; the unencompassable alterity at the very core of world beings that ultimately thwarts any representational closure or subsumption in thought. Heideggerian phenomenology pursued this core thematic and further circumscribed the adequacy of intellection as a dominant mode of engaging the world. Not through rejection or setting it aside, but by thinking *into* its heart, and touching the ground which first gives rise to the very possibility of distinguishing the rational and irrational. To the site, that is, where the categories which give sense to thinking and acting in any historical period first arise. Phenomenology thereby reveals that human being is more deeply implicated in the process of symbolic institution of the world than any reflexive powers of consciousness can order—and more, that human being has a deeper vocation in the ongoing process of world constitution than any philosophy can embrace, and any psychoanalysis can analyse or claim province over.

But, at the same time, post-Husserlian phenomenology showed that this vocation is not beyond the potential of a lived experience that is irreducible to any subjective happening. Phenomenology, as carried forward by Heidegger, ended up becoming practical: the traditional priority of theory over acting is inverted and their relations transformed. Heidegger showed why, under contemporary conditions, questions of making sense of our world, and what is worth contemplating and doing, all become contingent on the 'attainment' of a certain mode of being, a certain life practice. Which is to say that a manner of conducting everyday life becomes the necessary condition for grappling with what is at stake in the present.

This manner of comporting ourselves concerns the attempt to be attentive towards, to touch with our very being, the site of phenomenal differentiation and upwelling which is prior to any possible ascription of categories of the cognitive and practical. It is the abiding near that vicinity, among world beings, before their co-option into the fixity of identities. This is what Merleau-Ponty means when (in a Working Note in *The Visible and the Invisible*) he urges us 'to pass from the thing as identity . . . to the thing as difference; i.e., as always behind, beyond, far off'. Learning such a mode of relatedness and endeavouring to correspond with the world-bearings disclosed there, cannot leave us unchanged.

The 'I' has a modest role in this region of world constitution in that it is a 'vulnerability', as Lévinas says, which is the sensibility before all volition, action and affirmation of perceptual experience— a subjectivity beyond 'the adventure of cognition'. The subject is here not dissolved but finds humility because this 'I' always loses itself as it is on the verge of finding itself in the recuperation of self-consciousness. Thus always preceding self-possession by the ego, this vulnerability is only approached through the long and arduous process of learning to 'step back' from our historically elevated sense-of-self which retards and confines our experience, prohibiting a closer fraternity with world beings.

The experience of this abiding makes no claim for grasping a more accurate signification, for possessing a purer identity. It is outside any thematic showing. It is already a signifyingness prior to verbal signs and the systematic features of language identified by linguists—an 'intelligibility before the light' is how Lévinas expresses it. This abiding will always be compromised in the representational present because it can have no nominative form. Words betray it, but verbal language is kept more attuned, more honest, through, as it were, following in the footsteps left by this abiding. Can thought challenge this? The claim of phenomenology is that thought qua representation ultimately produces its own closure. Carefully pursued to its limit, the principle of reasonableness—that everything has an explanatory cause, a ground—is itself found to be groundless. Delimiting the domain of reason by following cognition into its own ground brings one to that 'mute realm of existence', to use Merleau-Ponty's fine expression, which silently but insistently calls for our responsiveness beyond any rational legislation. Phenomenology shows that the contemporary heightened sense-of-self and being-as-identity are correlates of the very structure of representational thought—a mode of relatedness which is progressively losing its relevance.

But is the philosophical 'overcoming' of representational thought a privileged or necessary path? This is the question René Char once posed to Martin Heidegger: 'Why should this ford of philosophy be only one stone?'. More than any philosopher before him, Heidegger knew that this realm may always have been better approached outside the academy, but also believed—as it seems a philosopher must—that thought needs to pursue its historical destiny towards the 'end of philosophy' (which is not a death or annihilation) before it can be transformed and turn more freely in the direction of that simple abiding.

It is, perhaps more than anything else, a characteristic of the present that what concerns us all, namely the potential for this simple abiding, is so obscure: thought tries to grasp the present situation, creating new schemas and more complex analyses, which ultimately result in greater fragmentation. This fragmentation breeds confusion and takes us further away from where we already are—if we have the simple patience and persistent attentiveness to approach in our everyday lives that ever-shifting field which gives every phenomenal appearing while moving nowhere itself.

It seems to me that the ambivalence I mentioned earlier concerning the French thinkers we have discussed in this volume ultimately turns on the double-faced nature of the grounding meanings made available by our (late modern) symbolic frame of reference, as it moves further into a phase of dissolution and reconstitution. I think that Derrida, Foucault and Lacan each manifest the ambiguity peculiar to our time—standing in the middle of an epochal transition which is not only a reconstitution of symbolic frames but the waning of a long historically dominant mode of engaging world phenomena.

Each of these thinkers exhibits a curious relation, and perhaps necessarily so, with the academy in terms of pursuing the full implications of their own thinking with regard to the status of thought and the cultural role of the intellectual vis-à-vis the question of practice. The hyper-reflexive prose, the shifting conceptual frames and frequent self-overturnings reflect the historical fate of a mode of thought accelerating towards not its demise but its supersession as the privileged mode of relatedness with the world.

In so far as recent French theory lends itself to assimilation by the academy as more grist for the knowledge industry mill, or is grasped at in cultural discourses and the arts by individuals essentially engaged in rationalising the fragmentation characterising their own life experience, then this work contributes towards perpetuating the regressive trends of a mode of symbolic institution which has outstayed its time. In so far as deconstruction, in its ontological rather than purely textual role, breaks up the rigid coalescence of world constitutive processes, and preserves the integrity of the site of appearing against being-as-identity, and its correlate, negative or non-being, it contributes towards the need of the present. Similarly, if 'liberating' the self from 'modes of subjection' by contesting power constellations or practising an 'aesthetics of existence' can in any way free the self to become more attentive to this domain, then it may nourish that other 'belonging-together' of human being and world. Or even if eliminating the *méconnaissances* (misrecognitions) of the ego and learning to listen to 'unconscious desire' can amount to more than a paradoxical affirmation of the dominant form of individuality, then the positive cultural role of such psychological practices may not pass completely unrealised.

But then does thought really require the addition of ever new supports if it is to steady itself before the experience of that abidingness that is already around us?

CHRIS MCAULIFFE

Some time ago Kevin Murray mentioned to me that his project had met with scepticism in certain quarters: the project would not be useful, it was suggested, because the fashion for French theory had passed. This attitude annoys me not because I am an epigone of French theory but because I am a historian. To dismiss ideas as fashionable is hypocritical in the extreme since it actually adopts the attitude that it condemns; that is, that thought is something trivial that flares and fades with the whims of fashion. For historians it is not a matter of consigning the spent fad to the dustbin of history but of asking why certain systems of thought carried such power, why this happened when it did, why the attraction faded. There is also a good deal of ignorant arrogance in such dismissals since many challenging authors remain virtually unknown in English circles—Alain Corbin, Sarah Koffman, and Christine Buci-Glucksmann are prime examples. That Baudrillard might have been a cult figure is not grounds for dismissal. On the contrary, he is part of the discourse of recent Australian art and therefore cannot be ignored. It seems to me that the following aspects of the consumption of Baudrillard in Australia ought to be explored in an effort to historicise his reception. I think we need to return to a moment in the early 1980s when a group of young artists and critics sought the tactical means to contest the exclusion of their art and their interests. Like many artists before them their means of self-definition and empowerment consisted of a kind of staged avant-gardism. That is, they acted out their difference tactically and rhetorically. They declared their interest in that which had been excluded: mass culture, photography, video, and performance. They sought ways of rhetorically declaring the passing of the discourses that excluded them: liberal humanism and marxism. Theory was used to underwrite this project. To a certain extent theory was used pragmatically, wherever and however it was useful in the struggle. Hence the tendency to read Baudrillard's texts as descriptive rather than speculative—to do so allows specific targets and concrete moments to be attacked and overturned. But by the same token deeper levels of understanding did develop, albeit in an ad hoc sense. Baudrillard's popularity might be understood in terms of the rhetorical and tactical parallels between his project and that of this avant-garde. Baudrillard, too, sought to counter his exclusion by lionising the forbidden—mass culture and media—and by rhetorically declaring the end of the reign of the doxa—orthodox marxist economics, humanism, and existentialism. The history of Baudrillard and Australian artists might lie in their common tactical purpose; that is, his antipodean epigones take up the spirit rather than the letter of his work.

JULIAN PEFANIS

I would like to start with a caveat—namely, that I wonder if it is not a bit homogenising to lump all these theories and their authors under the title of 'French theory'? For surely one of the remarkable features of the writers and thinkers we have discussed is the sheer volume and inventiveness of the ideas that they have, one way or another, mobilised; and I wonder if it does any of them any justice to conflate them like this? In addition, do we not leave ourselves open to the accusation that we are creating a cult devoted to a pantheon of proper names? Surely the usefulness of a particular theory comes about from its relevance to a particular situation rather than its generic characteristic as a panacea. But to put this caveat aside, and to speak in general terms, I would say that one of the most useful lessons of recent and contemporary French thought is that it teaches us to think and write in terms that are not strictly philosophical, and further, it demonstrates that this thought and writing can be a legitimate—even if not legitimating—and ethical means of appropriating the world.

Theory has traditionally been used as a type of 'black box'. Not like the black box that is fished out of the remains of an aircraft when it crashes (though this might be relevant in some cases—what went wrong with this system of thought?), but like the black box used in electronic engineering and design. In this case, when designing an electronic system, an engineer will sometimes require a component whose output and function is known, but whose internal structure remains otherwise obscure, undesigned and speculative. In the parlance of electronic engineers, this unknown but accounted-for component is called a 'black box'. I think that many approaches to theory follow this component design: it is valued or disparaged primarily for its known output, its use value, rather for its internal, speculative design or coherence.

On the other hand, I think what is particularly interesting about the more recent theory to emerge from France is the way that it actually resists these impulses to put it to use—either as a heuristic for textual analysis or as a paradigm for sociological or psychoanalytic analysis: it is simply too speculative, too literary. It is likely to short-circuit the systems to which it is attached. We would then need to reformulate our question: what is the use of fiction? Finally, to those who would declare the end of theory (which is surely only possible through an elision of its moment of seduction) I would remind them of another nominalist fallacy, perpetrated in Paris. This involved another black box, or more precisely, a 'black room' called *l'enfer* (hell) of the Bibliothéque Nationale. It was a room in which was kept all those documents, books and images which were, from one point of view or another, unspeakable, unviewable—anathema. Unrecorded and appearing in no catalogues, this material was *hors de circulation*. In the late sixties there were insistent demands that the contents of 'hell' be made publicly accessible in the name of the freedom of information. The truly archaic administration of the Bibliothéque resisted bitterly until one day when, with its back to the wall, it finally declared shamefacedly and disingenuously: 'Hell no longer exists'.

CLARE O'FARRELL

What use is French theory in Australia? Some would claim that in importing French theory we are merely exposing ourselves to a dangerous disease, what David Malouf describes as the 'chronic affliction' of the French 'pox in the head'.[1] Others would argue, however, that far from being a disease, French theory is a welcome remedy to the rigor mortis induced by prolonged exposure to the dessicated excesses of the Anglo-Saxon tradition.

French thought does in fact play a number of significant and vital roles in the Australian context—and not the least of these roles is a social one. Those who are interested in French theory in Australia form what Michel Foucault describes as a 'society of discourse'. As he remarks, the function of 'societies of discourse' is to preserve and produce discourses, but only within a closed space, distributing these discourses according to strict rules, so that the owners are not dispossessed by this very distribution.'[2] One recognises a fellow French theorist by the use of such secret passwords as 'discourse', 'differance', 'genealogy', 'deconstruction', among others. And, of course, there are the obligatory proper names—gods of a secret religion—enthusiastically and reverently invoked to ward off the evils of Anglo-Saxon empiricism, representation, and a dry academic style devoid of any suspicion of poetry. Not just *anybody* can enter this exclusive club. It is necessary to spend years agonising over obscure and mysterious texts at advanced hours of the night, learning how to reproduce a style sternly aimed at discouraging any rash young upstarts foolish enough to think they can force the doors of this club. In extreme examples, members may have been forced to learn French.

French theory also confers on its practitioner a revolutionary aura; one instantly acquires the much-admired status of 'subverter' of the status quo at minimal cost. Lengthy discourses on power, knowledge and regimes of truth need not apply to anything *too* specific, or require any further activity besides mouthing that one is undermining the accepted instances of power in discourse. But, if the best French theorists do in fact succeed in this aim, a number of their imitators are merely following very strictly codified laws of a well-established counter-culture. One also has the satisfaction of belonging to a noble and persecuted minority. As the French philosopher Jacques Bouveresse remarks with fine irony:

> The role of Cassandra obviously presents not unimportant
> advantages for the philosopher. It is always possible, indeed,
> indispensable, to present oneself as someone who *cannot* be heard,
> at the very moment when you are making the most noise. This
> technique is not a new one for philosophers. Althusser and his
> disciples, for example, proceeded by giving the impression of going
> heroically to war against an adversary superior in arms and
> numbers.[3]

In short, French theory in Australia, as elsewhere, fulfils all the functions of a social club, with its criteria of inclusion and exclusion.

So much for the social uses of French theory, now very briefly for its intellectual uses. As one critic remarks, for the Anglo-Saxons, 'no theory is better than a poor one, while [for the French], a poor theory is better than none at all'.[4] One of the major advantages of French theory is that it provides *ideas*, a way of making interconnections between different domains of knowledge, of seeing a general picture, something which is sadly lacking in more traditional Anglo-Saxon approaches.[5] To propose only one example: French theory can offer some valuable and unusual insights into some of the problems facing Australian academics and educational institutions at present. Both Jean-Paul Sartre and Jean-François Lyotard offer very plausible analyses of the shortcomings of any educational policy or view of intellectual endeavour which is too clearly tied to short-term economic and political aims.[6] At a more personal level, Bourdieu notes the predicament of the academic as an individual with large cultural capital and meagre economic capital and the kind of frustration this produces. Likewise, his remarks in *Homo Academicus* on the struggles for power and symbolic domination in universities are highly relevant to the Australian setting. François Bourricaud also notes the contradictory pressures to which intellectuals are subjected, as they try to juggle their conflicting roles as creators and researchers, and as teachers and members of increasingly state-regulated bureaucratic organisations (universities).[7]

These are but a few brief items to illustrate the point that one can valuably apply ideas and methods used in French context to the Australian situation. Of course, this transfer automatically entails a number of important modifications. In adapting French theory to Australia it is not enough to learn key words and dogmas by rote. It is a question of undertaking the difficult and painstaking task of research and reflection.

NOTES

1 D. Malouf 'Suffering the French disease' *The Australian* May 1978
2 M. Foucault *L'Ordre du discours* Paris: Gallimard, 1971, pp. 41–22, transl. 'Orders of discourse' *Social Science Information* 10, 1971, p. 18
3 J. Bouveresse 'Pourquoi pas des philosophes?' *Critique* 34, February 1978, p. 100
4 Paul Jorion 'Letter: "Le regard eloigné" ' *The Times Literary Supplement* 4 May 1984, pp. 495–96
5 For a more extensive discussion of this classic opposition between French 'rationalism' and Anglo-Saxon 'empiricism', see Clare O'Farrell *Foucault: Historian or Philosopher?* London: Macmillan, 1989, pp. 22–25.
6 J-P. Sartre *Plaidoyer pour les intellectuels* Paris: Gallimard, 1972, pp. 22ff; and J.-F. Lyotard *La Condition postmodern: rapport sur le savoir* Paris: Minuit, 1979; transl. as *The Postmodern Condition: A Report on Knowledge* Minneapolis: University of Minnesota Press, 1984
7 F. Bourricaud *La Bricolage idéologique: essai sur les intellectuels et les passions démocratiques* Paris: P.U.F., 1980, pp. 17–25. One has only to read *The Australian*'s Higher Education Supplement each week to observe these problems of economics and identity emerging with increasing clarity in the Australian intellectual setting.

INDEX

162